HIMU

The Hindu 'Hero' of Medieval India

(Against the background of Afghan-Mughal Conflicts)

Sunil Kumar Sarker

ATLANTIC

PUBLISHERS & DISTRIBUTORS (P) LTD

ATLANTIC
PUBLISHERS & DISTRIBUTORS (P) LTD

7/22, Ansari Road, Darya Ganj, New Delhi
Tel.: +91-11-4077 5252, 2327 3880
E-mail: orders@atlanticbooks.com
Web: www.atlanticbooks.com

Published by Atlantic Publishers & Distributors (P) Ltd.

Reprinted in 2024, 2025

Printed & bound in India by Atlantic Print Services

TO
MY DEAR WIFE
MRS. MANJU

(i) History is the "queen of sciences".

–Barani in *Tarikh-i-Firoz Shahi.*

(ii) "... There is no tribe so rude that has not attempted History, though several have no arithmetic to count Five."

–Th. Carlyle.

(Tennyson, G.B., *A Carlyle Reader*, Modern Library, New York, 1964, 55).

(iii) "We know only a single science, the science of history."

– Marx and Engels.

(Collected Works, Vol. 5, Progress Publishers, Moscow, 1976, 28 and R. Podolny, *Something called Nothing*, Mir Publications, Moscow, 1986, 15).

(iv) "All records, by their very nature, are liable to error – nay, they contain factors which make for error."

– Ibn Khaldun.

(J.N. Sarkar, *History of History-Writing in Medieval India*, Ratna Prakashan, Calcutta, 1977, 119).

Preface

Frankly, I was inspired to work on the present topic by the noted historian R.C. Majumdar's regret: "Neither fate nor historians have been kind to Himu ... Historians, medieval and modern, have scant justice to, and failed to show due appreciation of the unique personality and greatness of a Hindu who, during the heyday of Muslim rule in India, worked his way from a grocer's shop to the throne of Delhi, and, but for an accident in a battle which turned victory into defeat, might have founded a Hindu ruling dynasty, instead of the Mughals, in Delhi .... Majumdar has dwelt on Himu in only about 2316 words, in the Appendix to *The History and Culture of the Indian People* (vol. VII), edited by him. Perhaps the historian could not find time to write more about Himu. I therefore felt an indomitable urge to write up a history of Himu. While I had already covered a long distance in my researches, I came across Mr. Bharadwaj's thin work on Himu. But my zeal was not defeated thereby, rather I was enthused to find that after six years' of researches, Mr. Bharadwaj could reveal only very little about Himu. Further, Mr. Bharadwaj's book, as he confesses, is rather a biography (and not a history) of Himu. But history is never biography and so I have treated Himu against the historical background of Afghan-Mughal conflicts, and I may candidly say that I have improved upon, and added to, the previous knowledge about Himu.

I firmly believe that history is a science and so it should contain no inaccuracies and harbour no doubt; it should avoid subjectivity, biasness, and supernatural elements learnt from hearsay. Unfortunately, I have come across a lot of all these. For instance, Eliot's narration of Adil Shah's dream of a *darvish* before his move against the Raja of Andrum (Dowson, 67-68) and Erskine's story of Humayun's meeting with three persons – Murad, Daulat and Saddat – contains an element of supernatural element. Incidentally,

Mrs. Anne Flora Steel's (*India Through the Ages*) and Adolf Waley's (*A Pageant of India)* narrations of the same 'incident' of Humayun do not agree with Erskine's (*A History of India: Baber and Humayun*). Another instance of supernatural element in medieval Indian historiography is the story of rainfall due to loud noise of men and neighing of horses in the Siwalik hills (Eliot's Posthumous Papers in John Dowson's *History of India As Told By Its Own Historians*). Eliot writes that such supernatural 'events' occurred to the army of Marcus Aurelius when it was engaged with that of Marcomanni "in the barren mountains beyond Danube" (*ibid.*). To support his belief in supernatural 'events', he says that "In modern days, it has frequently been observed that severe actions have been followed by rain, and philosophical reasons have been assigned for this curious effect" (*ibid.*). (For Eliot it may be added that a heavy shower of rain followed the atomic blast in Hiroshima in 1945.) Another historian of eminence, Makhan Lal Roy Choudhury, also narrates, in his book *Akbar*, some supernatural 'events', that allegedly occurred during Akbar's time. We, certainly, cannot comfortably decide about the apodicticity of such supernatural 'events', nevertheless we can say that, as in history there should be no scope of fancy of hearsay, – and I suppose the source of most of these supernatural 'events', is hearsay – history should shun all these, on the plea that doubt always lurks over them. Perhaps we should always keep in mind Geyl's warning : "The discipline of history, the historical spirit, is a force for truth and against myth." (Jagadish Narayan Sarkar, *History of History Writing in Medieval India*, 139.)

Again, authentic historical writings sometimes contain gross inaccuracies. For example, Jean-Baptiste Travernier in his *Travels in India* says that Humayun "died in the year 1552" (and not in 1556, which is the truth). Still again De Laet Director of the East India Company, who had been irked at the "carelessness of the Indian historian" (*infra*), himself committed Himalayan blunders. For instance, he writes: "In the year of Christ 1550, or 960 Mahomedan style, Sher Khan or Sher Shah, the Pathan king and ruler of the whole of Hindustan *died of gout in the fort of Gwalior* leaving behind his son *Firoz Khan*, who was 12 years old" (Contemporary Dutch Chronicle of Mughal India) (*italics* mine). Historians should not be so careless, indeed!

However, I have tried to be objective, unbiased and free from prejudices and supernaturalism. Pronunciations of proper names are sometimes erratic. The abbreviated name of Hemchandra is spelt and pronounced variously – Hemu, Himoo, Himun (Elliot), etc. However, I have followed R.C. Majumdar and Lt. Col. Sir Wolseley Haig. I have avoided dia-critical marks. And in spite of my sincere and hard labour, I confess, I have not been able to go upto my expectation in this dissertation on Himu, and am remaining content keeping in mind the wise advice of Wassiljew: " 'The more deeply a scholar enters into a science the less does he remain content with his researches.' " (Augustus, *Emperor Akbar,* xlix).

Last but not the least, I am grateful to my friend Dr. K.R. Gupta, Managing Director, Atlantic Publishers and Distributors, for kindly publishing this humble work.

SUNIL KUMAR SARKER

Contents

	Preface	*vii*
1.	The Background	1
2.	The Afghan-Mughal Conflicts	24
3.	Steady Rise of Himu	35
4.	The Battle of Panipat, Death of Himu, and the Consequences thereof	57
5.	The Hindus *vis-a-vis* the Afghans and the Mughals	76
6.	An Assessment of Himu	101
	Select Bibliography	110
	Index	116

(i)	The family tree of Himu	35
(ii)	Emperors on the throne of Delhi	53
(iii)	The battle-array of the Second Battle of Panipat	61

CHAPTER I

Introduction or The Background

I

The history of Himu or Basanta Rai or Vikramaditya or Vikramajit or Hem Chandra is seductively interesting. Like Diocletan, who "began as a common warrior" and became an "emperor" (Korovkin, 234) and Sher Shah, who "blossomed out of dust" (Tripathi, 115), Himu was like a meteor. Himu originated in the horizon and pierced vertically through the medieval Indian sky, torn by the storm of Afghan-Mughal conflicts for supremacy; and instantly flashed across the apex, which event some contemporary Hindu dreamers might have wistfully construe as a sign of Hindu regeneration out of, or liberation from, five hundred years of Muslim attempt at subjugation, but which actually, as per a fiat of fate, did only one thing – it consumed Himu himself. Therefore, Himu's rise was meteor-like, and his fall even was not otherwise. Himu can be compared with Tilak who "was of humble origin, being the son of a baber, but was handsome, entertaining and accomplished, speaking and writing well both Hindi and Persian. From the service of Abu'-l-Hasan he had been promoted to that of Mahmud's minister and eventually to that of Mahmud himself" (Haig, 1965, p. 30). Himu's rise was as sharp as that of Aurelius who had been a private soldier but rose to the height of an Emperor (Weech, 228). Incidentally, there is resemblance between Gaumata, a priest, who seized power from Cambyses, son of Cyrus (Progress Publishers, 1985, p. 28), and Himu, who shrewdly snatched away the reign of the empire from the hands of Adil Shah, because Himu was also, as some say, of a priestly class. In fact history reveals many instances where people eating humble pie rose to the highest pinacle. Thus many of the rulers of the Delhi Sultanate were slaves in their early years, and thus Epictatus, the slave-philosopher, became a close friend of the Roman Emperor Hadrian (76 A.D.–138 A.D.) or Humayun's ewerbearer Jauhar had the peculiar luck of sitting on the throne of Delhi, though for a few hours. But, Himu, probably surpassed them all, in the sphere of wonder.

And, yet, this "romantic" figure, or let us say phenomenon, passed unnoticed by historians. The savant-historian R.C. Majumdar rightly complains : "Historians of India have so far done scant justice to his (Himu's – SKS) personality and achievement with the result that he is hardly known to Indians to-day as *a remarkable and distinguished person during the Medieval Age*" (emphasis added) (Majumdar, 1984, p. XV). Majumdar called Himu a "Hindu hero" (*Ibid.*), and himself did some laudable endeavour for "rescuing from oblivion the name of Himu or Hemchandra" (*Ibid.*). Perhaps Majumdar could not find sufficicient time to write up a full account of this great personality. This present dissertation aims at just the same.

Of recent years, an unsuccessful bid to write the history of Himu has been made by Mr. Ram Kanwar Bharadwaj. His six years of researches have produced *Hemu : A Critical Study of the Man and his Work* (Bharadwaj, 1975), a thin work of only about 77 pages (including references, etc.). But this book suffers from the following grave flaws :

1. As per the wish of the author, it is a mere "biography" (p. v) of Hemu. It has only very narrow historical perspective. But history is not biography, or, as Thomas Carlyle writes in his essay "On History", "the essence of innumerable Biographies" (*Tennyson*, 57). Thus Limburg-Browner's *Akbar* is a novel and not an historical work (*Augustus*, p. xlv).

   It may be noted here that Tagore's (Datta, 1980, p. 277) and Tolstoy's (*War and Peace*, Part II) concept of history is too inclusive and philosophical. However, our idea of history does not exclude the possibility of writing history concentrating on a single person, but then it must be written from some historical point of view. Thus, for example, the following are not exactly biographies :

i. *Mahadji Sindhia – A Political Career in India, 1730-1794* by Mr. A.S. Agaskar (awarded Ph. D. by Bombay University).

ii. *Nana Phadnavis and the External Affairs of the Maratha Empire, 1742-1800* by Yashwat Narayan Deodhar (awarded Ph. D. by Bombay University).

iii. *Delhi Under Mahadji Sindhia* by Mr. Krishna Nand (awarded Ph. D. by Delhi. University).

iv. *Nana Phadnavis and the Internal Affairs of the Maratha State, 1742-1800*, by Mr. Srikrishna Vithal Gokhle (awarded Ph. D. by Bombay University).

v. *Mir Jafar* by Mr. Atul Chandra Roy (awarded Ph. D. by London University).

(Datta, 1957, pp. 20-49.)

vi. *Shujauddaula* by Dr. A.L. Srivastava (vol. I awarded D. Litt. by Agra University and vol. II awarded D. Litt. by Lucknow University).

vii. *History of Shahjahan*, by Mr. Banarsi Prasad Saksena (awarded Ph. D. by London University). in 1931.

viii. *Narayan Guru as a Social Educator*, by Mr. Gerald G. Pereira (awarded Ph. D. by Kerala University) (*Indian Dissertation Abstracts*, Vol. XV, No. 1, 1986, pp. 64-65).

2. Mr. Bharadwaj, unfortunately, has not consulted many very important works of highly authoritative Western historians, such as Rawlinson, Haig, Briggs, Thomas, Steel, Waley, Walpert, Stewart, Travernier, Erskine and Hunter, as is apparent from the body of the text and the bibliography of only 34 titles.

3. The work has done scant justice to the dimension of the fight for might among the Afghans, Hindus and the Mughals (Chagatai Turks). Certainly this was the back-drop of the stage in which Himu played the most blazing role.

4. The description of the battle-formations and the progress of the 2nd battle of Panipat, where Himu received his defeat, is too sketchy in the work.

5. Mr. Bharadwaj referred to certain unauthoritative (historical) sources. For example, he referred to the poetic works of

R. Sankrityayana. The picture of Himu, printed in the book, is not trustworthy. The picture shows Himu to be stout, riding on horse-back and wearing a sword. But the noted historian Iswari Prasad writes that Himu was "*too feeble to sit on horse-back and never wearing a sword*" (emphasis added) (Prasad, 1956, p. 190).

Briefly, the work has dwelt with Himu only as a man (because it is avowedly a "biography" and not a history) and not as a spear-head of the Hindu-Afghan combine against the Chagatai Turkish bloc. Its gaze is very narrow, and for wanting a social perspectival leverage, it can hardly be called a work on history. Barani rightly says that history is "no mere narration of events in the biographical setting" (Mukhia, 1976, p. 19). We should judge Mr. Bharadwaj's work from this wise angle. Besides, the work adds very little to the knowledge about Himu, to be found in the text-books; and regarding the language, argumentation and the mode of presentation of materials, the work is not neat. However, we have incorporated in this dissertation whatever substantial material Mr. Bharadwaj has presented in his book, and withal mention credits to him at appropriate places. It should be admitted here that R.C. Majumdar's short note on Himu is certainly laudable. Nevertheless, we should not remain content with that much, but strive for a full-scale historical portrait of the hero and his time. The present dissertation aims at just that.

R. C. Majumdar regretfully complained : "*Neither fate nor historians have been kind to Himu...... Historians, medieval and modern, have done scant justice to, and failed to show due appreciation of, the unique personality and greatness of a Hindu who, during the heyday of Muslim rule in India, worked his way from a grocer's shop to the throne of Delhi, and, but for an accident in a battle which turned victory into defeat, might have founded a Hindu ruling dynasty, instead of the Mughals, in Delhi ...... (For), There is no doubt that he furnishes the only shining example of a Hindu, born and brought up as such in a Muslim State, who once dominated the political stage of Northern India by sheer merit and personality without any advantage of birth or fortune*" (italics mine) (Majumdar, 1984, p. 97). And with these words Majumdar concluded his "short sketch" of "Himu – A Forgotten Hindu Hero" (*ibid*). Majumdar is to be gratefully thanked for two short notices on Himu – one in

The History and Culture of Indian People : The Mughal Empire, and the other in his *Military History of India*.

The history of Himu is almost buried in mystery, because :

i. The Contemporary historians were mostly Muslims, the majority of whom were averse to writing about 'infidels' and Himu being an 'infidel' escaped their eyes.

ii. With Himu's head being severed by the Mughals off his body at the mighty stroke of a sabre, the Afghan influence in India was puffed off. The vanqiused Afghans and Hindus forgot their hero and busied themselves in their day-to-day life, while the Mughal victors took only a miniature view of Himu and so cared not for entering his exploits in their royal Tarikhas at appropriate length.

iii. Almost all the contemporary literature was a-historical.

iv. No genuine interest, unfortunately, has so far been shown in Himu by modern historians.

II

A Little digression on historiography in general, and medieval Indian historiography in particular, may receive indulgence here. Thomas Carlyle in his essay "On History" rightly wrote that "there is no tribe so rude that has not attempted History, though several have not arithmatic enough to count Five" (G.B. Tennyson, 55) and S. Radhakrishnan in his essay "The Meaning of History" said that Herodotus wrote "so that time may not blot out the memory of human achievement and so that the great and remarkable deeds (perhaps like those of Himu – SKS) of the Greeks and the barbarians may not lack their need of honour" (Radhakrishnan, 135). But the history as recorded by historians is never absolute and unchangable. And, therefore, Anatoly Rakitov, in his *Historical Knowledge*, writes : "Each generation, it is said, rewrites, history anew through the prism of its notions, passions, and expectations, and its social sympathies and anti-pathies." (Rakitov, 18). History is one of the most complicated subjects of inquiry and so Rakitov suggests, appropriately, the systems-epistemological method for historical knowledge. Historical knowledge involves the problem of historical truth. Rakitov writes: "The study of methods of establishing truth in general is the main problem of the theory of knowledge (in historical inquiry – SKS)" (*ibid* 76). "Textual familiarity with the works of Herodotus shows that he was extremely worried about the possibility of his stories and historical information. Thucydides, too, put the truth of his exposition above his many other merits. Thus, the fathers of historical science were aware right from the start of the problem of the truth of historical knowledge ...." (Rakitov, 78). Rakitov is quite right in asserting that historical knowledge is dynamic. There are philosophers of history who deny the scientific character of historiography. Schopenhauer, Windelband, Ricart and Gurerich are such philosophers. Gurerich, for example, said that "Attempts to know the 'objective' by abstracting the 'subjective factor' in history signify nothing else than a merciless disfiguring of the living organism of human culture on a procrastean bed of natural science thinking" (Rakitov, 119). But most philosophers of history as well as historians sided with the scientific theory of historiography by asserting that historical knowledge is descriptive. But such descriptions must be socially significant. Rakitov writes: " .... historical knowledge, and description as its basis, single out, as their main subject, *The development and change in socially significant human activity, and the latter is inseparable from consciousness*" (Rakitov, 167). Here, Rakitov, perhaps, by 'consciousness' means the social consciousness of the co-eval social matrix. However, incidentally, we may recall to mind that Mr. Bharadwaj's *Hemu* lacks in this aspect of historiography.

While describing facts the historian must have an eye on the motivation of the individuals or group of individuals engaged in events. Lappo-Danilevsky, in consonance with Windelband and Rickart, and Zimmel's psychologism, writes : "By historical fact in its most characteristic, specific meaning, the historian mainly means the effect of the individual on the milieu." (Rakitov, 177). But Sir. Karl Popper does not admit of individuality in historical knowledge. According to him, "History is essentially a chronicle of political and events" (Rakitov, 217). Perhaps Mr. Bharadwaj has missed Popper's point.

The main problems of historiography are three: the epistemological problem of the knowledge of the past, the problem of objectivity, and the problem of value or of morality. According to R.F. Atkinson, the knowledge of the past is available through direct observation, memory and testimony. But direct observation may be wrong observation or mal-observation. Secondly, human memory, particulary the memory of the people in general is very short. And thirdly, testimonial sources suffer from personal equations and motivations. Therefore, the historian should always be on his guard. The second main problem of historiography is objectivity. Atkinson is quite right when he says : "Objectivity worries thus arise at different levels and are not all of them of the same sort, in that different considerations bear on them, although a good many have a common source in the idea that selection necessarily compromises objectivity; that selection is inevitably arbitrary, or biased by the historian's personal prejudices, or by his value judgements, which it is presumably taken for granted are wholely subjective and/or arbitrary too" (Aktinson, 70). However, in spite of the wariness of the historian – Atkinson is pessimistic here – the whole truth in history is unattainable. Atkinson writes: "The probability of making true statements about the past is by general consent insufficient to guarantee objective history, which few are content to conceive as simply a matter of stringing together true statements about a topic. There must, at the very least, also be selection and summary, not say interpretation. And it is here that the real doubts about objectivity arise. It is feared that in making their selections historians will be expressing their personal and class prejudices, their moral, political or religious attitudes; that what purport to be accounts of the past are shaped less by what happened then than by influences operative in the historian's present" (Atkinson, 73). And the third and last main problem of historiography is valuation. Practically, history can never be absolutely value-neutral. Atkinson is of the opinion that "value judgements must be admitted to the subject matter of history." (Atkinson, 189). This is so because "historians are not commonly deficient in keen human sympathies – if anything, the reverse" (Atkinson, 190). But who will be the 'subject' or judge of this moral evaluation of historical events or facts? A.J.P. Taylor writes : "I ought perhaps to have warned the reader that I do not come to history as a judge; and that when I speak of morality I refer to the moral feelings at the time I am writing about (We will remember this when we shall deal with the question of morality pertaining to Himu's assuming the title of Vikramaditya and declaration of independence – SKS)" (Taylor, 7). Atkinson also favours a value-neutral approach to historiography. On the contrary,

Lord says that "pronouncing moral verdict is central to the task of history" (Atkinson, 198).

But whose moral judgement is it – of the individual or of the society ? Atkinson here writes : "Manifestly historians are interested in individuals and their actions and, so far as this goes, there is no reason why they should not pass judgements upon them. But, still more obviously, historians are concerned with social matters too; notoriously the individuals to whom they pay attention have to be of social significance" (Atkinson, 200).

Now, with these considerations about general historiography, let us deal at some length with some of the features of the historiography of medieval Indian period. It may be assumed that medieval Indian history sprawls from the 13th century (The foundation of the Delhi Sultanate) down to the beginning of the British rule in the 16th century. (But opinions differ.) However, medieval Indian historiography suffers from all the shortcomings of general historiography. In addition, it has some special features and limitations. These may be summarised as follows :

(i) *Official Records and Court Bulletins :*

a. Pre-Mughal historiography was extra-Indian in inspiration and methodology, but Mughal historiography was, for the most part, Indian in inspiration and methodology. And yet the all India character of Mughal historiography is not to be found. For example, the Mughal historians bore a quantum of hatred towards Deccan. Jagdish Narayan Sarkar Writes : "Mughal historians, official or private, had a supreme contempt for rulers of the Deccani Shia (The Mughals were mostly Sunni – SKS) Sultanates who were styled not as Kings or Sultans but only as Zamindars, duniadars or marzbans" (Sarkar, J.N., 45).

b. It was also anti-Hindu in attitude. Badaoni, for instance, G.B. Malleson writes point-blank, was a "bigotted Musalman" (Hunter, 90).

c. Lastly, Mughal historiography sometimes was didactic.

(ii) *Non-Official or Private Historians (and Biographies) :* Mulla Abdul Qadir Badauni (1540-1615) held history to be a science, but himself being religiously very much inclined, his works were limited in their appeal. Mulla Muhamad Qasim Hindu Shah, surnamed Ferista (1570-1623) was not free from sectarianism and bigotry. On the other hand, though Ram Sharma called Khafi Khan the "Prince of Plagyrists" (*Sic*), yet, perhaps, he was one of the few impartial historians of his time, as it can be glimpsed from his praise of Shivaji : "... The Maratha leader strictly prohibited harm to 'Mosques, the Book of God, or Women' " (Sarkar, J.N., 117). His *Muntakhab-u'l-Lubab* or *Tarikh-i-Khafi Khan* is invaluable for the history of Mughal India.

Ibn Khaldun counted the sources of historical errors. These are partisanship towards a creed or opinion, overconfidence, failure to understand, mistaken belief, inability, desire to gain favour, ignorance of the laws governing the transformation of human society, exaggeration, and ignoring the transformations that occur in the condition of epochs and peoples with the passage of time and the changes of periods. In fact, almost all the indigenous historians of the Mughal India were the victims of one or more of these vices. Again, medieval Indian historiography has sometimes been propagandistic, as is, to some extent, evident from Abul Fazl's *Akbarnamah* (Sarkar, J.N., 127). Medieval Indian historiography also suffers from critical attitude and acumen. "The Indo-Moslem historians have been accused of being recorders first, researches afterwards. Their methods of studying history were comparable to those of studying 'hadis' (tradition) written from authority" (Sarkar, J.N., 130). Another drawback of the historiography of medieval India was, according to Grunebaum, a tendency towards hero-worshipping and particularity. Grunebaum writes: " 'The weakness of Arabic historiography is its concentration on personalities and on military incidents and court cables.' ... One can hardly expect to find an independent political theory of study of the social forces of the age where everything was conceived as depending on God and His decrees" (Sarkar, J.N., 131).

As against Ibn Khaldun, K.A. Nilakanta Sastri and H.S. Ramanna, in their *Historical Method in Relation to Indian History*, have enumerated four kinds of errors often committed by historians – didactic error, patriotic error, partisan error and an error that Langlois and Seignobos call 'Froude's disease'– a sort of constitutional error (Sastri, 1956, pp. 12-15).

Historical method comprises four parts : heuristic, criticism, synthesis and exposition. The present thesis has been mostly heuristic though the three other 'parts' have had adequate leverage. Leo Tolstoy divided historians into three categories – biographical, universal and cultural (He also spoke of a fourth category – philosophical). Though this dissertation falls in the category of biography (in the broad Tolstoyean sense), yet it is something more than that. Tolstoy said "history is only a science" (Tolstoy, 1312), but Sastri and Ramanna are not far from truth when they say that "History as a subject of study is more or less completely at the mercy of its sources" (Sastri, 1956, 35). However, if Indian history is to be based on a scientific foundation, all of the errors innuendoed to above should be relegated to the limbo, and *voila ce qu'il faut*! And let us conclude this section with the words of Qizerman : "All history needs to be studied afresh!" (Qizerman, 19).

III

The history of Himu is inseparably bound up with the history of Afghan-Mughal conflicts. Mr. Bharadwaj certainly committed a great blunder by ignoring, or at least drastically minimizing, the importance of this fact. India being an adjacent country of Afghanistan, it was only natural that the high-lander Afghans freely entered the plains of India in quest of wealth and livelihood, of selling services, etc. But they came to India mostly in the train of the invaders from the north-western part of the Indian subcontinent – from Turkey and the neighbouring countries. At the beginning, the Afghans could not wield any power in India, and they could not do so till the beginning of the Lodi dynasty. Gradually, they got recruited in the different armies of the warring monarchs. After the Delhi Sultanate, the Khaljis and the Tughluqs ruled over Delhi and the neighbouring areas. Next, the Sayyaids came to power. These people are said to be coming from Arabia. The last Sayyaid King, Ala-ud-Din Alam Shah, was an incompetent ruler and so could not safeguard the dynastic legacy that Muhammad Shah left for him in 1443. It was during this time that the Lodis snatched the sceptre from the Sayyaids away. Ala-ud-Din had a treacherous *wazir* in collusion with whom one Bahlul Lodi, an Afghan and the governor of Sirhind, occupied Delhi in 1451.

The Lodi Afghans were not strangers to India. They "were enrolled in large numbers in the army of the Delhi Sultanate in the second half of the thirteenth century. Some Afghan nobles played an important role during the Khalji and Tughluq periods. The Afghans constituted an important section of the *sadah amirs*. A large number of Afghan Zamindars emerged in Firoz Tughluq's time. There were concentrations of Lodis at Multan and Sirhind." (Banerjee, 233). It should be remembered that the Khaljis were not real Afghans. "The Khaljis were generally regarded as Afghans, although they were really Turks. They lived for many years in the Garmsir (hot region) of Afghanistan and naturally adopted some Afghan manners and customs" (Banerjee, 197). In the same way, the Tughluqs were also Turks, of humble origin. By the by, the "careful scholar" Edward Thomas erroneously called the period from about – 1200 to 1526 the period of the "Pathan Kings". But Sir Wolseley Haig writes in the Preface to the third volume of *The Cambridge History of India* thus : "Of the five dynasties which occupied the Throne of Delhi during this period, from about 1200 to 1526, three were Turkish, or of Turkish descent; one claimed to be of Arab blood; and one was Afghan, but probably not Pathan" (Haig, 1971, p. V).

So, the Sultanate dynasty, the Khalji dynasty and the Tughluq dynasty were Turkish in origin; The Sayyaids *claimed* to be coming from Arabia; and only The Lodis were Afghans. Percival Spear, in his *A History of India* (Vol. 2), gives a pen-picture of the Afghans. We may quote from him here at some length with profit : "The sceptre of the Turk in northern India, so rudely broken by Taimur, had now been grasped by the Afghans. These men were chiefs and adventurers who had migrated to India to take service with the Turks in the preceding centuries; had received grants of land for their services, and had used the post-Timurid confusion to hoist themselves into political power. Their strength was energy, courage, and vigour; their weakness pride, clan spirit, and an inability to work together. Daulat Khan Lodi (1451-88) had gradually built up a new power at Delhi, but he was rather the President of a noble confederacy than an absolute monarch in the old style. His son Sikandar (1488-1516), who lived in Agra, followed in his footsteps, but when the grandson Ibrahim tried to reassert the royal prerogatives, trouble began. His followers became restive and disloyal. The Lodi Afghans (their tombs and mosques may be seen in Delhi to-day), ruled from the banks of the Indus over the Punjab and Uttar Pradesh to the borders of Bengal. They stopped short at about the river Chambal to the south and had no hold over Rajasthan. Their empire had become impressive in size but it lacked inner strength. It had no independent source of authority and exercised no bureaucratic control. It was essentially a coalition of landed Afghans controlling other landholders, Muslim and Hindu, by virtue of their united military power. Disturb the sense of conformity, very easy in the case of Afghans and the whole fabric became unstable. This was what the luckless Ibrahim did. Bengal, once a province of the Delhi Sultanate (*Sic*), was now an unstable splinter Kingdom of Afghan chiefs" (Spear, 16-17). These Afghans, from the very beginning of their incursion wanted to stave off the Turks. But, ultimately, the Afghans had to give the place of prominence to them. Afterwards, the Turks, particularly the Chagatai Turks, snatched away the reign over almost the whole of northern India and they kept the Afghans under subjugation. Nevertheless, the Afghans were never completely wiped off the Indian scene, as is evident from the fact that even during the fall of the Mughal empire, the Afghans once again tried to assert their power.

Another branch of the Afghans was the Sur Afghans. Compared with the Lodi dynasty, the Sur dynasty wielded more power and exhibited more exploits in the Indian arena. The Lodi Afghans were trying to seize the throne of Delhi, albeit unsuccessfully. It was Bahlul Lodi who for the first time captured the throne of Delhi from the Sayyaids in 1451. The Lodi Afghans were serving the Sayyaids, but they "were adventurers and fortune seekers and had little reason to feel any sense of loyalty or respect for the imbecile Sayyaids. These adventurers had spread over the southern, Central and Eastern Punjab and infiltrated into the heart of the U.P. where they acquired large fiefs" (Tripathi, 20-21). With the help of the Afghans of Roh, Bahlul Lodi made a dent, though temporarily, in Northern India. Bahlul meticulously adopted a catholic policy in administration, and yet his rule was not free from racial, tribal and parochial considerations. Bahlul's son, Sikandar Lodi, succeeded him in 1489, and his grandson, Ibrahim Lodi, ascended the throne of Delhi in 1517. Both of them had to face insurgency, internally, and aggression, externally. During Ibrahim's rule, Hussain Shah and Nusrat Shah were hatching a pre-emptive attack on Southern Bihar. In the western sector, Rana Sanga spread his influence upto the eastern part of Rajputana. At that time, from the north-west, Babur, the sixth King in the Timurid line, had been contemplating gate-crashing into India. *This tripartite conflict is not to be lost sight of. India was then a bone of contention among the Hindus, the Afghans, and the Turks. But, unfortunately, historians so far have narrowed down this tripartite conflict into a bipartite conflict, i.e., only the conflict between the Afghans and the Turks. We shall come to this point a whit later on.*

For the present, let us deal with the Turko-Afghan conflict. During the time of Ibrahim Lodi, a conflict between the Afghans, who were, so to say, *naturalised Indians*, and the Mughal (Chagatai Turk) foreigners was inevitable (The word 'Chagatai' is derived from the name of Chagatai Khan, the second son of Chingiz Khan). In 1519, consolidating his position in and arround Farghana, Babur crossed the Indus and in the next year conquered Bhera and threatened Sialkot and Saiyadpur (Aminabad). He also laid claim over districts of Khushala, Chinab and Chiniut, saying that these districts were snatched away by the Afghans at the time of the death of Ulugh Beg Mirza, his uncle. On the other hand, Ibrahim Lodi extended his father's Kingdom of only Lahore eastwards upto Bihar where the Lohanis were very strong. In the north, Ibrahim's empire sidled the Himalayan ranges, and in the south it included Alwar, Biyana, Dholpur, Gwalior and Chanderi.

Daulat Khan was not in good terms with Ibrahim, though both were Afghan Lodis. Daulat wanted somehow to rule over Lahore independently, like a King. In fact, it was his house that had disposed the Mughals of the Western Punjab. However, he did not want to get embroiled in conflicts with either Babur in the western sector or with Ibrahim Lodi in the eastern. But yet, he got entangled in the conflict. Earlier, Daulat Khan kidnapped the envoy of Babur, but, soon peace was established. Finding Ibrahim Lodi an incorrigible tryant, the Afghans of Lahore sought Babur's help to dislodge Ibrahim. At this time there was a simmering dissatisfaction between the Hindus (Rajputs), led by Rana Sanga, and the Afghans, led by Ibrahim Lodi, regarding the eastern portion of Rajputana. Consequently Rana Sanga also invited Babur's intervention.

Finding the two most powerful allays on his side, and perceiving internal conflicts among the Indians galore, Babur touched off, in December, 1525, his fifth invasion of, what he loosely termed in his *Memoirs*, Hindustan. In the Punjab, Daulat Khan submitted to Babur. Alam Khan Ala-ud-Din, uncle of Ibrahim Lodi, also appealed to Babur for his invasion. "Babur took Lahore from Ibrahim's troops which had been sent against Daulat Khan. He then captured Dipalpur. Daulat Khan realized the danger and ceased to support Babur" (Sastri, 1986, 443). This was certainly an act of treachery on the part of Babur. Daulat Khan earlier invited Babur to make a common cause against Ibrahim Lodi, but Babur, immediately after capturing Lahore, sent troops against his own collaborator. Perceiving the treacherous act of Babur, Rana Sana, who earlier contemplated allowing Babur to attack Ibrahim Lodi, provided Babur helped him to capture the eastern part of Rajputana in return (Rana Sanga and The Lodis were at daggers drawn on the question of Rajputana), withdrew his invitation to Babur and extended his help to Ibrahim Lodi, instead. In November, 1525, hearing that the Uzbegs had besieged Balkh, Babur went to Kabul, but hurriedly returned to India with less than 12,000 men to fight against Daulat Khan who avoided confrontation by capitulation and died soon after. Thus Babur hamstrung the Afghans. Next, on April 21, 1526, he met Ibrahim Lodi in the first battle of Panipat, giving out as the main cause of his fight the cause of Islam. Incidentally, in the same year Islam spread upto Hungary under the leadership of Sulaiman, the Magnificent, or as the Osmanlis honourably called him, the Legislator (Brockelmann, 291-294). However, Ibrahim Lodi died in the field of Panipat with 15,000 men, and Babur occupied Delhi and Agra. He won India as swiftly as Alexander the Great won Europe, but like Sultan Mahamud he did not come to India for forrays, but settled here to plant the third contesting force (Mughal) in India.

IV

The Mughals are the third force because prior to their coming to India, there were already two other forces – the Hindus and the non-Mughal Muslims. Historians, so far, have committed two mistakes – one of commission and the other of omission. Firstly, they have taken the non-Mughal Muslims and Mughals into account as a monolithic Muslim bloc. So much was the difference between the Afghan natives and the Mughal foreigners that the period from the time of the Delhi Sultanate to that of the British should not be called the Muslim period of Indian history, basing the periodization on religion only, but the whole period should be divided into Afghan rule and Turkish rule. Due to the partisan motivation of the historians of the house of Taimur and their object of glorifying the Mughals, the history of the Afghans, who ruled India for about 106 years, has not received due justice of being adequately noticed. The historians have mistakenly thought the struggles for overlordship between the Afghan and the Mughals during the medieval period are intra-bloc conflicts. This is far from the truth. The Mughals should not be equated with the Afghans, because the former were quite different from the latter in almost every respect, good or bad. The Afghans were self-seekers, quarrelsome, indisciplined, and maintained low ambitions. The Mughals, on the other hand, were disciplined barbarians, blood-hungry, and, nursed very high ambitions. The entry of the Afghans into India was slow and almost imperceptible, and as such there was less resistance from the natives against their immigration. And in course of time the Afghans were "Hinduised" (Marx, 30), but the Mughals, till then, remained foreigners, strangers. Even in the thirteenth century, the Mughals were "inhuman and beastly (wrote an English monk), rather monsters than (humans – SKS), thirsting for and drinking blood" (Davis, 404), and were even "a threat to the existence of Islam" (*ibid.*, 405).

True, there were struggles between the Hindus and the Afghans, but the tension did not mount on the medium of religion. On the other hand, the Mughals, from the very beginning of their entry into India, had a religious zeal against the native idolaters, as is evident, for instance, in the oratory of Babur before his troops just on the eve of the first move in the field of Panipat (1526), or as is evident in the purpose of Taimur, the forbear of Babur, in chastising the Hindus for their idolatry, and the Muslims of India for their conniving at it. Not only this, the Afghans as well as the Khaljis were always on the alert against the Tatars, the Turks and the Mughals. As early as in 1260, during the reign of Nasir-ud-Din, a Mughal mission from Hulagu put to the sword about 12,000 men, women and children, who were not only Hindus but also Afghans. Balban, the successor of Nasiruddin had a hard time to stave off the Mughal menace. "Mongol (Mughal – SKS) danger was ever present and Balban kept his army trained and disciplined to the highest pitch of efficiency. The threat of the Mongols was checked by refortification of Lahore in A.D. 1270. Balban's cousin, Sunqar was ever ready to meet the attack of the Mongols ....." (Sastri, 1986, 347). After the Delhi Sultanate, Jalaluddin Firuz of the house of the Khaljis continued the anti-Mughal measures. "Against the Mongols who invaded India in A.D. 1292 the Sultan (Jalaluddin – SKS) was somewhat firmer. Many were put to the sword after a crushing defeat, 'though by the terms of the final peace, those who did not leave India were allowed to settle in the neighbourhood of the capital and swell the ranks of the New Muslims as the converted Mongols came to be called'. " (Sastri, 1986, pp. 349-50). Ala-ud-Din taught the Mughals a great lesson when in 1299 his general Zafar Khan routed about 200,000 Mughals in the battle of Kili. That the Mughals were psychologically anti-Afghans is clear from the attempt of the New Muslims, who were Mughals, to rise against Ala-ud-Din whose fiat left 30,000 New Muslims (Mughals) dead in one day in Delhi. Next, Ghias-ud-Din took the task of Ala-ud-Din. "In his five years' reign he was occupied in strengthening the defences of the north-west frontier to keep back the Mongol (Mughal – SKS) hordes, ..." (Sastri, 1986, 358). And next, Sultan Bahlul Lodi, the Afghan, fought five times with the Mughals and thus repulsed them.

All these well-groomed defence measures, however, were not always perfect, for in the autumn of 1398 Timur or Tamerlane, a Barlas Turk and *amir* of Samarkhand, marched upon Delhi with an army 90,000 strong. Mahmud, the grandson of Firuz Shah, fled away and *Timur was proclaimed the King of Delhi*. Soon after, Timur, of his own, went home, and an interlude in the series of Mongol inroads followed. After a gap of about 121 years (from 1398 to 1519), Babur made his first attack on India and occupied Bajaur. Then, after five invasions, Babur at his sixth defeated Ibrahim Lodi in 1526 (April) and occupied Delhi and Agra. Nevertheless, there was no dearth of zeal among the Afghans to keep the Mughals off the country. After Ibrahim Lodi's death in the plain of Panipat in 1526, the Sur clan of the Afghans raised its standard against the Mughals. The Lodi Kings constituted the first Afghan dynasty and the Sur Kings the second. The Sur Afghans were also intermittently harassed by Mughal inroads, so much so that Sher Shah Sur, in his dying regrets confessed : " 'I have three of four desires in my heart, which will remain without accomplishment, and cannot be eradicated except by death. One is, I wished to have depopulated the country of Roh, and to have transferred its inhabitants to the tract between the Nilab and Lahore, including the hills below Ninduna, as far as the Siwalik; that they might have been constantly on *the alert for the arrival of the Mughals,* and not allow any one to pass from Kabul to Hind, ... Another is to have entirely destroyed Lahore, that so large a city might not exist on the very road of *an invader*, where, immediately after capturing it on his arrival, he (Mughal leader of invaders – SKS) could collect his supplies and organize his resources. Another is, to have built two fleets of fifty large vassels each, as commodious as *sarais* for the use of pilgrims from India to Mecca; ...... the last is, *to have raised a tomb to Ibrahim Lodi in Panipat,* but on the understanding that opposite to it there should be another tomb of the Chaghatai Sultans, whom I may have despatched to martyrdom; ...." (emphasis mine) (Dowson, 143-44). So we find that the non-Mughal Muslims and the Mughals were the two contending forces for overlording India.

V

The third contesting force, so far dealt with by historians at a low key, was the Hindus. Since when the Arabs had been in touch with south-western part of India on maritime trade, we do not know. But the Muslims came to govern India, we may say, since 712. Muhammad-bin-Kasim, son of Chach, was "the Arab invader" (Sastri, 1986, 247) who, after the death of Harsavardhan, had slain the Brahmin ruler of Sindh, Dahir, and himself became the governor of that province. This usurpation was local and so the Hindu population of India did not take cognizance of it. Further, after the death of Harsavardhana, India fell into pieces of petty Kingdoms, and so the harm caused to Sindh could not raise a national protest. The Muslim occupation of Sindh was treated as a petty affair by the Hindus. However the whole of India, except Sindh, was ruled by the Hindus. The peninsular India was under the overlordship of Narasimhavarman. In the north-east, Bengal had been successively ruled by the Guptas, Palas and Senas, till Lakshman Sena was overthrown by the Muslims. The ancient Hindu Kingdom of Kamarupa owed allegiance to the Guptas. Assam successfully frustrated all the Muslim attacks down the ages. Kanauj was efficiently ruled by Yasovarman, but his successors being weak, Shihab-ud-Din or Muhammad Ghuri conquered it in 1194. The vast land track from Kanauj in the north to Kathiawar in the west and to Ayodhya in the east was ruled by the Gurjaras, Rajputs, Pratiharas, Gahadvalas, Chahumans, Maitrakas or Valabhis, Chaulukyas, Paramars of Dhara, Chandellas, Chedis and others. On the other hand, the penninsular India was ruled by the Chalukyas, Rastrakutas, Pallavas, Pandyas, Cholas, Bijjala Kalachuris, Hoysalas,

Kakatiyas and others for centuries. All these were Hindus and so we can say that before the coming of the Muslim power to India, *i.e.*, before the dawning of the medieval period, India was absolutely Hindu India.

From the very beginning of the Muslim invasions in India, the Hindus put up resistances, though in vain because of the prevailing disunity among themselves. Historians generally ignore the fact that there was always an anti-Muslim attitude, the degree varying from time to time and from place to place, prevailing among the Hindus. "The Indian states suffered defeat several times in the field of battle and lost extensive territories, but this did not mean the end of their well-developed culture. The buoyant spirit with which the Hindus rose as often as they bent low has won the admiration of historians" (Sastri, 1986, 327). And this spirit of the Hindus of fighting away the Muslim foreigners, though not in a concerted way, stood in the way of the Muslims of conquering the whole of India in a huff. This attitude of the Hindus is not to be lost sight of and though this attitude gradually diluted later on, it never evaporated, as we find it present during the whole of the medieval Indian history. But, one thing is perhaps true : during the Delhi Sultanate, and before, the Hindus were not so much prejudiced about the religion of the invaders – they did not see the invaders as much as Muslims as mere invaders. But the attitude of the Hindus towards the invaders during the Mughal period was different : they saw them more as Muslims than as mere invaders.

However, before the coming of the Mughals, we find two contesting forces – the Hindus and the Afghans. But after their entry into India three powers were contesting among themselves – the Hindus, the pre-Mughal Muslims and the Mughals. However, when the Mughals were pouring into India the Hindus and the Afghans (the pre-Mughal Muslims) made a common cause against the Mughals. Yet even there the Hindus were somehow not unconscious about their identity. Thus Himu should not be looked at only as the Prime Minister of Adil Shah, but also as an objective correlative of the subdued Hindu spirit that continuously struggled to overthrow the superimposed Muslim hegemony, and that it could somehow find in Himu a vent to raise its head once again, though only to be puffed off instantly, and this for decades to come.

The pre-Mughal Afghan Muslims, due to their long habitation

in India, merged themselves into the mainstream of Indian life. So, they were now no more foreigners, but natives. Hindu-Muslim communal rivalry was at its nadir in Northern India during this period. No doubt there was some sort of rivalry, but it was political in nature and not communal. But in the peninsular India, the picture was different. There they were contesting on the communal line, and yet this ill-will at the top did not in any way obviate social harmony between the two communities. Curiously enough, both the Hindus and the pre-Mughal Afghan Muslims regarded the Mughals (Chagatai Turks) as enemies and they fought the latter sometimes hand-in-hand. J.L. Mehata writes that many of the Indian rulers, Hindu and Muslim alike, "enjoyed popular support of their subjects in their struggle *against Babar and his successors*" (italics mine) (Mehta, 60).

In the 16th century, almost the whole of Northern India was ruled by the Muslims, because though the Sultanate as "an Islamic state" (*ibid.*) declined, the political power of the Muslims did not abate. However, the political map of the pre-Mughal India could be delineated as under :

(i) Provinces Under The Hindus

During the pre-Mughal period the Hindus had only four provinces under control — Mewar and Marwar (modern Jodhpur) in the north-west, Orissa in the east and Vijoynagar in the south. When Babur was gate-crashing Northern India, Orissa had been ruled by Prataparudra Deva (1497–1540). "For a very long time this state served as a wedge between the Muslim states of Bengal and the Deccan and exercised a check on the penetration of Muslim influence into the south from the south of Bengal" (Mehta, 66).

In the north-west the two Hindu states of Marwar and Mewar were very strong, particularly the latter one. Within two years of Ala-ud-Din Khalji's conquest of Chitor, the Sisodia Rajputs reconqured it. This "signalled a general uprising in the region against the *Sultanate* which resulted in the emergence of many new Rajput principalities; Mewar and Marwar were the most prominent among them" (Mehta, 67). The Rajputs of Marwar fought valiantly against Sher Shah during the reign of Maldeva (1532–1562). But the Sisodia Rajputs of Mewar were the most powerful. Rana Sangram or Rana Sanga (1509–1528) of Mewar was a legendary ruler and warrior who bore as many as eighty marks of wounds on his person and had lost one leg one arm and one eye in the battle-fields. Rana Sanga came into conflict with at least two pre-Mughal Muslim rulers. In the south-west of his Kingdom, he defeated Mahmud II of Malwa and in the south-west he did not permit the Sultans of Gujrat to extend their sway over Malwa or Rajputana. The Rana also defeated Ibrahim Lodi who wanted to step on the soil of Rajputana.

In the peninsular India, Vijoynagar (modern Madras, Kerala and parts of Mysore and Andhra) was a very powerful Hindu Kingdom with an appreciable height of cultural development. Vijoynagar was founded by Harihar and Bukka Rai who were probably Kinsmen and revenue officials of King Pratap Rudra Deva II, the Kakatiya ruler of Warrangal. They were captured by the Turkish army of Muhammad-bin Tughluq but were released by the King and engaged as imperial agents of Delhi. Soon they returned home to fight for the liberation of the south from Turkish domination. In 1336 they founded a habitat in the hills and forests on the bank of Tungabhadra and named it Vijoynagar. In its north was Madura which was conquered by Bukka Rai. "The rulers of Vijoynagar championed the cause of Hinduism *albeit* they adopted their non-Hindu subjects." (Mehta, 71). Rana Raya, the plenipotentiary Prime Minister of Sadasiva, the last Hindu ruler of Vijoynagar, entangled himself in the suicidal conflict of succession in the Muslim Bahmani Kingdom, neighbouring Vijoynagar, with a view to gaining some benefit. He was a Hindu fanatic and so was hated by the Muslim population of Bahmani Kingdom. At last the Sultans of Ahmadnagar, Bijapur, Golkunda and Bidar — all Muslim splinter states of Bahmani Kingdom — made a common cause against Vijoynagar and destroyed it in the battle of Talikota (25 January, 1565).

In the east, Assam was another Hindu state. The Ahoms, a Shan tribe, occupied Assam in 1228. "Assam is notable for its unique success in maintaining its independence against Muslim attacks" (Sastri, 1986, 252). It surrendered only to the British in 1825. Raichur Doab was also an independent Hindu principality (Davies, C.C., 42).

(ii) *The Provinces under the Pre-Mughal Muslims*

The pre-Mughal Muslims ruled twelve big and some small states. In the extreme north, Kashmir was under the Delhi Sultanate. Shah Mirza, an inhabitant of Swat, overthrew the Hindu ruler of Kashmir in 1339 and ascended the throne of Kashmir under the title of Shamsuddin Shah. In 1420 Shah Khan occupied Kashmir and ascended the throne under the title of Zainul Abedin. For his measures of catholicity in favour of the Hindus, such as abolishing the Jizia, banning cowslaughter and patronizing Sanskrit, he was affectionately called the "Akbar of Kashmir". However, towards the close of the fifteenth century, Kashmir experienced anarchy, and consequently in 1585 Akbar annexed it. Before this, the mountainous state remained almost isolated from the rest of the country.

In the south-east, Sultan Firoz Tughluq founded Jaunpur on the bank of Gomti in the memory of his cousin Jauna Khan (Sultan Muhammad bin Tughluq). Sultan Mubarak Shah, the adopted son of Malik Sarwar, founded the Sharqi dynasty of Jaunpur. Hussain Shah (1458–1500) of Jaunpur invaded Delhi but was repulsed by Bahlol Lodi. In the long run Jaunpur was conquered by the Lodi Sultan and Hussain Shah fled to southern Bihar. Bahlul Lodi placed his son Barbak Khan on the throne of Jaunpur. For some time, Jaunpur "retained the separate identity of the Kingdom in subordinate association with Delhi" (Mehta, 65). In the central part of India, Malwa was conquered by Ala-ud-Din Khalji in 1305 and it remained under the Delhi Sultanate till 1398 when its governor, Dilawar Khan Ghori, established the Ghori dynasty. Malwa had always been torn by internecine quarrels among the Muslim nobles. Taking this as an opportunity, Rana Sangram Singh of Mewar defeated Mahmud II of Malwa. Malwa was again conquered by Sultan Bahadur Shah of Gujrat in 1531. It was once again overrun by Humayun in 1535 (or 1536) and was annexed to the Mughal empire. In the west, there were two Muslim states — Gujrat and Sindh. Gujrat became virtually independent of Delhi under its governor Tafar Khan, son of a Hindu convert, who assumed the title of Muzaffar Shah. Sultan Bahadur Shah of Gujrat conquered Malwa in 1531 but within some four years Bahadur Shah was thrown out of both Malwa and Gujrat by Humayun. However, taking the advantage of Humayun's negligence and incompetence, he recovered Gujrat. Bahadur Shah fell a victim to the treachery of the Portuguese who drowned him in the sea in February, 1537. His successors, though weak, continued to rule till 1572 when Akbar annexed Gujrat. Sind was another Muslim state in the west. It remained under the Delhi Sultanate for many years. Its first independent ruler was Jan Khairuddin who established the Sumra dynasty in Thatta. In 1520, Shah Beg Arghun captured Sind and founded the Arghun dynasty there.

Khandesh, a small *iqta* under the Delhi Sultanate, was situated in the south of Gujrat. Malik Nasir (1399–1438) of Khandesh conquered the fort of Asirgarh from its Hindu chief. The rulers of Khandesh being weak, some of its territories were annexed by its neighbours and in course of time Akbar conquered Asirgarh in 1601.

In the far east, the Muslim province of Bengal was a constituent part of the Delhi Sultanate from its inception. Later on it was divided into eastern and western parts, the eastern part being ruled by Fakhruddin Mubarak Shah from Sonargaon, and the western part by Haji Ilyas from Lakhnauti. In course of time Haji Ilyas annexed Sonargaon and ruled over the whole of Bengal under the title of Sams-ud-Din Ilyas Shah. Ilyas was succeeded by Jadu. The fifth descendent of the Haji dynasty was murdered by Barbak Shah, an Abyssinian slave in 1486. Consequently, Bengal experienced anarchy for some time and ultimately Ala-ud-Din Hussain Shah, a Bengali noble, laid the foundation of the Hussaini dynasty. Hussain Shah's son, Nursat Shah whom Babur described as a capable and powerful monarch, ruled from 1518 to 1533.

In the south, just north of Vijoynagar, was the Muslim state known as Bahmani Kindom. Hasan Gangu laid the foundation of this Kingdom in 1347 with its headquarters at Gulbarga. The Kingdom had 18 Sultans who ruled for 180 years, from 1347 to 1527. Muhammad Shah III got his famous and capable minister, Mahmud Gawan, killed and so after Muhammad Shah III's death his 12 years old son could not keep the Kingdom united and consequently the Bahmani Kingdom split up into five splinter states of Bijapur, set up by Yusuf Adil Shah, a Turkish noble; Berar; Bidar; Ahmednagar and Golkunda.

Thus we find that at the time of Babur's invasion, there were already two contesting forces in India – the weaker Hindu force and the stronger pre-Mughal Muslim force. The communal tension between the Hindus and the Muslims was appreciably low, but it still persisted. In the Muslim states the Hindus had to pay *Jiziya* which they sometimes thought, was humiliating, though often they accepted this tradition as a *fiat accompli* without bearing any grudge. Proselytizing into Islam went on, but not with so much of zeal as the Mughals showed. The feeling that the pre-Mughal Muslims were foreigners was not present, yet, sometimes, as in Vijoynagar during the time of King Rama Raya, communal feelings reigned supreme. The Muslim rulers sometimes could not relegate to the limbo the Quranic injunction of turning any *dar-ul-harb* into *dar-ul-Islam*. The pre-Mughal Muslims comprised mainly the Afghans, the Turks or the Turko-Afghans. All these peoples originally were (before settling in India) nomadic and barbarous. Karl Marx wrote : "Arabs, Turks, Tartars, Moguls, who had successively overrun India, soon became Hinduised, the barbarian conquerors being, by an eternal law of history, conquered themselves by the superior civilization of their subjects" (Marx, 30). But actually it was not to be so "soon"; at least before the coming of the Mughals, the pre-Mughal Muslims were not so civilized. Thus there was a great difference between the nature of the Hindu society and that of the pre-Mughal Muslim society. And so, the two societies should not be taken into account as just one society. However, there was much cohesion between the two societies, so much so that they built themselves into one bloc to obliterate the foreign Mughal Muslims' entry into India.

Since the capture of Sind by Muslims, the Hindu power had certainly been diminishing, but still it was looking for an opportunity for revival. The strivings of the Hindus for revival have been scattered and irregular. In the north, such strivings were apparent, for example, in the three Hindu leaders — Rana Sanga, who fought against Babur; Himu, who fought against Akbar, as King Vikramaditya of Delhi; and, later on, Shivaji, who fought against Aurangzab, for a Hindu Rajya. In the south, though Vijoynagar was a contented Hindu state, yet some of its rulers wanted to expand its periphery. During the reign of Adil Shah Sur, the Hindus were quite oblivious of the existence of the Greater India and her achievements of the ancient times; nevertheless, from time to time, the Hindus wanted to put off the pre-Mughal and Mughal Muslim yokes, alike. The life and achievements of Himu are a document of a temporary and local Hindu revival, within a long chain of such others.

CHAPTER II

Afghan-Mughal Conflicts

We have seen that in the first half of the 16th century, three forces (and not two, as historians generally tell us) were contesting for possession and power — the organized Mughals, the unorganized Afghans, and the equally unorganized Hindus. The Afghans were not Pathans, says William Hunter in his *Preface* to Wolseley Haig's *The Cambridge History of India* (Haig, 1965). According to him "Of the five dynasties which occupied the throne of Delhi during this period, from about 1200 to 1526, three were Turkish, or of Turkish descent; one claimed to be of Arab blood; and one was Afghan, but probably not Pathan" (*ibid.*). However, though Himu belonged to the Afghan forces, he was a Hindu, and it is clear from circumstantial evidences (we shall discuss these in the next chapter) that he wished to found a Hindu Kingdom by converting the Afghan force into a Hindu force without the ceremoney of proselytizing. In fact, by moving cautiously and slyly, he could materialize his dream, though for a while — he sat on the throne of Delhi, assuming the title of Vikramadıtya (The title of an ancient Hindu King who ascended the throne ın 56 B.C.) and stood against Akbar as such.

To materialize his favourite dream of establishing a Hindu state (he, of course, could not wish it in early life) by fishing in the muddled water of Afghan-Mughal conflicts. That the Hindu power was not completely wiped off India before, is certain. In the previous chapter we have seen that there were at least four Hindu provinces in India, at the time of Babur's invasion. Augustus vouchsafes that even after the battle of Khanwa (1527), the Rajput (Hindu) power, "The proud spirit of this noblest of India's races long remained unbroken" (Augustus, 46). Augustus continued : "The day when they were lords of India was indeed long past but men of the mould of Sanka and high-spirited comrades could neither forget nor forgo the time of their earlier supremacy" (*Ibid.*, 45). James Tod unconsciously has shown his sympathy with the Rajputs, or for that matter, probably, with the whole of India, when he has written : "Can a nation which has run its long career of glory be regenerated? Can the soul of the Greek or the Rajputs be re-animated with the spark divine which defended the Kangras or Chitore or the pass of Thermopylae? Let history answer the question" (Tod, 255). Himu was an inhabitant of Rewari, Hariyana, which is not far from Rajputana of the glorious Rajputs. So, it is possible that he was aware of the past glories of the Hindu Rajputs and also of their romantic dream, nursed with the inner regards of their hearts, of establishing a resurgent Hindu State by over-throwing the foreign Muslim domination. And Himu was half-lucky in establishing a Hindu State by occupying the throne of Delhi, in the muddled politics of Afghan-Mughal conflicts, by over-throwing the Mughals and putting an end to the "Pat'han usurpation" (*ibid.*). So, to understand better how a man of the street could rise to the stature of a King of Delhi, we should, perhaps profitably, follow the Afghan-Mughal conflicts of the time.

It was then the second Afghan or Sur power (the first being the Lodis) that ruled the roost in Northern India, during the time of Babur and Humayun, that the Afghan-Mughal conflicts continued and these came to a stop in the Second Battle of Panipat. Historians generally do not enter in the text books the second Afghan (Sur) dynasty in the chronology of the Kings of Delhi. Further, they do not recognize Himu as a King of Delhi, between Humayun and Akbar. This is a gross misrepresentation of facts. Again, they neglect the chronology of the Sur dynasty. For instance, historians do not tell us definitely when the second Afghan empire began functioning, though they tell that it ended in 1560 when Sher Shah II was defeated by Akbar's general Khan Zaman Uzbek in Bengal. All this is due to the fact that the medieval Indian history has so far mostly been written *from the perspective of Mughal chronology* and as such Hindu and Afghan (non-Mughal) elements have not received due attention from historians.

The Sur rule may be said to begin from 1534 when Sher Khan defeated Jalal Khan Lohani, son of Bahar Khan, of the Lohani Afghans, at the battle-field of Surajgarh. But actually, Afghan-Mughal conflicts occurred even before that. Sher Shah, *nee* Farid, was the son of Hasan, the *Jagirdar* of Sassaram. Sher Shah served under Bahar Khan Lohani, the ruler of Bihar, under Babur; and then under Jalal Khan Lohani, son of Bahar Khan Lohani and Sher Shah's own pupil. After his *marriage de la convenance* with the beautiful Lad Malika, widow of Taj Khan or Tajkhan Sarang Khani (after the latter was murdered by his eldest son by another wife), owner of the fortress of Chunar, on the bank of the Ganges. Finding him growing in power, Humayun marched against him in 1531. Sher Shah bought time by temporarily acknowledging Humayun's overlordship. In the meantime Jalal Khan Lohani marched against Sher Shah and met him at Surajgarh and established the rule of the Sur dynasty in 1534.

There were four powerful Afghan tribes — the Lohanis, the Lodis, the Surs, and the Karranis. The first Afghan dynasty (the Lodis) fought with the Mughals upto 1526 when Babur routed them for ever. The Lohanis were undisciplined. During the reign of Ibrahim Lodi (1517–1526), they, under the leadership of Dariya Khan Lohani, raised the standard of revolt against Ibrahim Lodi who sent Nasir Khan Lohani to suppress the revolt. Nasir Khan, contrarily, himself revolted against Ibrahim Lodi. However, "After the death of Dariya Khan Lohani, his son Bahadur Khan declared himself the Sultan of Bihar with the title of Muhammad Shah and struck coins in his name. The other nobles (these nobles were Lohanis and they showed obeisance to Ibrahim Lodi – SKS) flocked to his court and the ranks of his armed forces swelled to over one Lakh. Ibrahim Lodi could do pretty little against the rebels and the eastern half of the Kingdom, including the erstwhile state of Jaunpur was cut off from Delhi." (Mehta, 63). So we find that The Lohanis were not a very weak sort of people.

The Lohanis made another serious effect to bring the Sur administration into trouble during the time of Sher Shah. After his defeat in the battle of Ghagra on May 6, 1526, Sher Shah and Jalal Khan submitted to Babur who restored them to their former statures. When in 1530 Dudu Bibi died, South Bihar virtually came under the rule of Sher Shah, because he acted as the regent of Sultan in his minority. "At this stage, the Lohani nobles made a serious effort to oust him from power but Sher Khan firmly stood his ground. He was prepared to share power with them but they did not agree. Instead, they got hold of the boy Sultan and fled to Bengal in order to secure the support of its ruler Nusrat Shah against Sher Khan whom they regarded as the usurper. Sher Khan was left with no other alternative than to assume the reign of government as an independent ruler of

South Bengal. He, however, refrained from adopting any high-sounding title and styled himself simply Hazrat-i-Ala" (Mehta, 123). Therefore, we find that the Lohanis were of no help in building an Afghan empire. The Karrani Afghans could not rise to prominence during the reign of the Sur Afghans. It was only after the death of Sher Shah that the first Karrani Afghans came to power in Bengal and Bihar, which earlier were the strongholds of Sur Afghans. After Sher Shah's death, Sulaiman Karrani proclaimed independence in Bihar. He then annexed Bengal and Orissa and put up headquarters at Tanda, but in 1568 he was humbled by Akbar. After Sulaiman's death in 1572, the Afghan nobles prevented his son Bayazid from mounting the throne and put up on it Daud Karrani, instead. Daud declared himself King and stopped sending messages to Akbar as was agreed upon by Sulaiman. To punish him, Akbar sent Khan-i-Khanan Munim Khan. Daud initially submitted but he attacked Munim Khan on his way back. Akbar, furious as he was, took the command in the first person and met Daud at Patna and defeated him. Daud fled to Orissa from where, after Munim Khan's death, he tried to retrieve his suzerainty, but was killed in an engagement with the Mughals near Rajmahal on August 12, 1576. With his head being sent to Akbar as a barbarours trophy, Bengal lost her independence of Delhi.

So we see that excepting the Lohanis, all the three other main and powerful Afghans fought with the Mughals without respite. But it was the Sur tribe that took the most prominent part in the Afghan-Mughal conflicts. Babur had sent Humayun to subdue the Afghans, which the latter successfully did. But when Babur himself was engaged in exacting loyalty from the Rajputs, the Sur Afghans of Bengal and Bihar were organizing themselves under Nusrat Shah for a show down with the Mughals. Meanwhile Mahmud Lodi, younger brother of the late Ibrahim Lodi claimed the throne of Delhi for himself. Ultimately at the confluence of Ghagra and the Ganges, Babur defeated the combined forces of the Lodis of Northern India and the Surs of Eastern India, on May 6, 1529. The battle of Ghagra is important for the fact that it showed the utter hostility between the Mughals and the majority of the Afghan forces in India.

Babur died on the 26th of December, 1530. He could not consolidate his power and only temporarily subdued the Afghans. After his death, the Afghans again raised their standard of rebellion and wanted to chase the Mughals away from India. Bahadur Shah of Gujrat paved their way by snatching away Chitor from Nasiruddin Muhammad Humayun. The Afghans of Bengal and Bihar saw in this defeat of Humayun his terminal decapacitation and so marched against Humayun under the leadership of Mahmud Lodi of Bihar, but they were completely routed by Humayun in the battle of Dawrah or Dadra or Dawrua in October, 1532. R.P. Tripathi writes : "In spite of the neutrality — rather treachery — of Sher Khan which caused great confusion in their army, the Afghans fought bravely but lost the battle. Two of their best leaders, Ibrahim Khan Yusuf Khail and Bayazid Farmuli were killed. Mahmud Lodi fled to Bihar and retired once for all into private life" (Tripathi, 70). In the battle of Daurah Sher Shah kept neutrality because he thought that the gains of the battle would go not to himself but to Mahmud Lodi and his company. Here, certainly, Sher Shah betrayed his self-seeking motive and so he cannot wash his hands of the charge of treachery. Sher Shah was certainly a "combination of faithful service and cold blooded treachery" (*ibid.*, 59). Yet, some historians are of the opinion that Sher Shah's neutrality saved the Afghans from mass destruction. However, after some time, Mahmud Lodi again contemplated an attack on Humayun and so reached an understanding with Bilban, Bayazid and other Afghan nobles of Bihar. Therefore, Tripathi, perhaps, is not quite right when he says that after the battle of Daurah, Mahmud Lodi "retired once for all into private life" (*supra*).

Mahmud and his collaborators compelled Sher Shah to offer his services for the cause of the Afghans. But the sly Sher Shah privately thought that such a move would cause the leadership of the Afghans slip off his hands. So he consolidated his power and captured the fort of Chunar. Humayun laid seize on Chunar, whereupon Sher Shah bought time by temporarily showing obedience to Humayun, verbally; and being thus pleased, Humayun retired. Meanwhile, Humayun suppressed the Afghan uprising led by Mahmud Lodi of Bihar. Humayun now turned to Gujrat. Bahadur Shah of Gujrat gave shelter to the Afghans. Taking this as an act of abetment, Humayun charged upon Bahadur Shah. Now, finding Humayun engaged in the west, Sher Shah marched upon Bengal and occupied the territory between Kiul and Sarkigali, from Sultan Mahmud Shah of Bengal. He then proceeded towards south-east and laid seize on Gaur. Humayun should had attacked Sher Shah in collusion with the *nawabs* of Bengal. Instead, he occupied Chunar after six month's battle. Hearing that Sher Shah had captured Gaur, Humayun marched to the capital of Bengal, Gaur. On his approach, Sher Shah left Gaur to the fate of Humayun without any fuss, with a view to capturing Jaunpur, Benares, etc. Indolent as he was, Humayun was relaxing at Gaur with potions of opium, his favourite treat, renaming the old capital *Jinnatabad* or paradise.

Sher Shah moved like hurricane and conquered the vast tract of land from Jaunpur to Kanauj. When he heard of this appaling tiding, the royal opium-eater came to his senses and moved forth towards Delhi; but on the way Sher Shah gave him a battle at Chausa in 1539 and routed him utterly. Next year, to avenge his defeat, Humayun met Sher Shah in battle array at Bilgram (battle of Kanauj, 1540), but again was humbled by Sher Shah, and consequently all the territory, Humayun earlier lorded over, came under Afghan sway. Sher Shah next annexed Sind and Multan, and moved towards Bengal in order to suppress the revolt there. Again, coming back to the western theatre, he conquered Gwalior and Malwa and occupied the fort of Raisin. Unopposed, he moved towards Mewar where Rana Maldeo submitted to him on approach. In this way, he extended his empire from Azmir to Abu. In 1545 Sher Shah laid seize to the fastness of Kalinjar where he died in an explosion while supervising an operation, on 22 (or 23) May, 1545 (Saturday) (11th Rabi 'ul awal, 952). For some time the news of his death was kept a secret as in the case of Humayun, his adversary (Mulla Bekasi acted as Humayun).

Vincent Smith opines that "if Sher Shah had been spared he would have established his dynasty, and the 'Great Moghuls' would not have appeared on the stage of history. His (Sher Shah's – SKS) right to the throne was quite as good as that of Humayun" (Sarkar, 1942, 47). Sher Shah "became the *de facto* ruler of the territories 'bound on the west by the bend of the Ganges from Kanauj to Chunar, on the south by the hills of Jharkhand (from Rohtas to Birbhum) and by the Bay of Bengal, on the east by the hills of Assam and Chittgong, and on the north by the Himalayas.' He legalised his conquests of the sword by formally assuming the royal title (Khan being changed into Shah) and ordering the coins to be struck and the *Khutba* to be read in his own name" (*ibid.*, 39). As a result of his victory at the battle of the Ganges or Bilgram, commonly known as the battle of Kanauj (17th May, 1540), "the throne of Delhi passed into the hands of the Afghans, and the Mughal Emperor (Humayun – SKS) was reduced to the position of a helpless fugitive" (*ibid.*). Sher Shah "had long set before himself the task of uniting the Afghans for the expulsion of the Mughals. This end he pursued with a cool and calculated patience, looking neither to the right nor the left, always watchful, always cautious, never resting" (Prasad, 59) and he thought that "it would be no hard task to drive these foreign Mughals from Hindustan ......" (Steel, 161). The animus between Humayun and Sher Shah was partly due to the fact that "while Humayun was a foreigner, Sher Shah's family, a frontier one by origin, had lived in the heart of India for three generations" (Sarkar, 47). Really, what Gascoigne says about Babur perfectly applies to Humayun as well. Gascoigne writes that during the last years of his life "Babar still regarded Kabul as his home province." (Gascoigne, 24).

Sher Shah reigned for only five years. He left at his death two sons – the elder of whom, Adil Khan, was lazy and prone to luxury, and "preferred obscurity to prolonged battle for the crown, and after a while disappeared and was no more heard of" (Steel, 162). The vindictive second son, Jalal Khan who had been to Rewah at the time of Sher Shah's death was proclaimed King under the title Islam Shah, "mispronounced Salim-Shah" (*ibid.*).

Tripathi here does not agree with Mrs. Steel. According to Tripathi, Islam Khan's elder brother, Adil Khan, almost immediately after the latter's ascension raised the standard of rebellion and dashed upon Agra. But the rebellion soon subsided when Khawas Khan joined Islam Khan. Islam declared that " 'he was that day constituted Emperor' when Khwas Khan had joined him." (Tripathi, 143).

Thinking that so long as Adil Khan was at large, security was not assured, Islam demanded homage from Adil Khan who sought protection under Khawas Khan. Islam fought the combined forces of Adil and Khawas at Marhakar, a small town near and west of Agra, and defeated them both. It may be said that here *Tripathi is more reliable than Mrs. Steel.* Adil is no more heard of only after this.

Khawas Khan again rose against Islam, being filliped by Azam Humayun, but Islam was providentially saved. Islam now attacked the Niazi Afghans who did not show loyalty to him. He routed them upto the western border of Ambala. The Niazis took the protection of the Ghakkars. From the Ghakkar country they wanted to enter Kashmir but was opposed by Mirza Haider Doghlat sent by Islam Shah. A fierce battle was fought in which Azam Humayun and his wife fought heroically and then succumbed to injuries. The Niazis, including women and children, were brutally treated by Islam Shah. "The most repugnant and disgusting feature in the Niazi war was the beastly treatment given to the Niazi women. Some were kept exposed for months in a state of nudity. Others were made over to harlots! Sher Shah's molestation of the Rajput women pales into insignificance before the cruel treatment given to Niazi Afghan women by Islam Shah" (Tripathi, 147). This fact is very significant because it shows that however much cruel Islam might have been, one saving grace of his was that he was not religiously so much bigotted.

Islam Shah continued to fight against the Mughals, but not with so much verve and deftness as his father had. He had some difficulties also. The insurrection of the Mahdi sect led by Ilahi caused him much trouble; so much so that the Mahdis followed even "pertinaciously disrespectul manner to the King" (Steel, 163). Islam Shah, almost immediately after ascending the throne went beyond the Sutlej and there, for reasons not clearly known, when Kamran, the estranged brother of Humayun, sought Islam's help for overthrowing Humayun. Kamran was received by Islam Shah "very coldly" (*infra*) and so "suspecting foul play, he (Kamran – SKS) fled in the guise of a woman into the Gakkar country" (Prasad, 187). This fact also betrays an instance of the negative relationship between the Afghans and the Mughals.

Hearing that Kamran ensconced himself in the Gakkar country, Humayun taking help of Shah Ismail of the Safavid dynasty of Persia, marched towards the Gakkar country to teach Kamran a lesson. This prompted Islam's action against Humayun, the Mughal. Islam Shah is also "said to have meditated carrying out his father's scheme of destroying Lahore so that the town could be of no service to the *invaders* (Mughals – SKS). (italics mine) (*infra*). "Islam Shah apparently designed to transfer the capital of the Punjab to a strong new fort which he had constructed at Mankot, on the exteremity of the Sewalik mountains" (Prasad, 188). This project of Islam Shah was also in accordance with the dying wishes of his father – to take some measures against the invasions of The Mughals.

The Mahdi movement, initiated by Shaikh 'Alai, was suppressed by Islam Shah. Ilahi or Shaik 'Alai was captured and a number of lashes, at the third of which he succumbed. Soon after, Islam Shah died of fistula on 30th October, 1553. But according to Abul Fazal,

Islam died "from a malignant ulcer which formed in one of his lower members owing to the issue of corrupt matter." (Abul Fazal, 616). According to Wolseley Haig Islam Shah died on 22nd November, 1554 (*Cambridge History of India*). Before Islam Shah's death, there were two attempts on his life for his cruelty to the Niazis and the Afghan soldiers – one in the Punjab and another in Gwalior.

Islam Shah, though mediocre, not only maintained his father's empire for 8 years, 9 months and 9 days, but also extended its boundary "by annexation of East Bengal and the establishment of his sway over the Kashmir valley" (Mehta, 136). At the time of his ascending the throne, the Afghan nobles tried to put hurdles on his way. His "brief fanatical contest with his elder brother" (*The Cambridge Shorter Hist. of Ind., p. 336*) caused disaffection among the Afghan nobles. The Niazi Afghans also rose against him. Nevertheless, despite his ill-treatment, the majority of the chieftains remained loyal to Islam Shah.

During this period, the power of the Khalji Turks and the Lodi Afghans was exhausted. Therefore the contest for supremacy now was between the Sur Afghans and the Mughals. Throughout his reign of eight years, Islam Shah waged constant battle against the Mughals. Yet, it was during his time that the second Afghan empire had gradually becoming ramshackle. Shuja'at Khan of Malwa proclaimed independence, and Taj Khan, a member of the Karrani tribe of the Afghans, occupied the throne of Bengal (1564). Yet, by and large, it was the Afghans that dominated Northern India. It was only after the death of Islam Shah in 1553 that the Mughals, under the leadership of Humayun, could raise their heads. However, *it was this Islam Shah that picked up Himu and placed him on a comfortable administrative position* – that of the superintendent of the Bazars.

"According to his (Islam Shah's – SKS) will" (*Akbar Nama*), his son Firoze or Firuz ascended the throne. Almost immediately after the ascension of Firoze, a ghastly palace incidence took place. On the very third day of his reign (there is a controversy – *infra*), Firoze was murdered by his uncle, Mubariz Khan, son of Sher Shah's younger brother, Nizam Khan. Mubariz was the brother of Firoze's mother, Bibi Bai (*vide* the genealogy of Sher Shah in the appendices). Mubariz Khan, immediately after murdering Firoze, ascended the throne and assumed the name Muhammad Adil Shah. His claim to the throne was contested by two of his brothers-in-law – Ibrahim Khan and Sikandar Shah; but the strongest opposition came from the former. He drove away Adil Shah from both Delhi and Agra and declared himself "Emperor of India" (Mehta, 136). Sikandar Shah who was previously the Governor of Lahore, occupied North-West India and declared himself independent. On the other hand, Malwa and Bengal revolted. This internal conflicts of the Afghans gave an opportunity to the Mughals. Humayun, with the help of a battalion that he received from the Emperor of Persia, occupied Punjab. In return, he gave the Emperor Kandahar. Humayun next occupied Delhi and Agra. Thus Humayun, in 1555, re-established himself as the Emperor of India, after a crownless state of fifteen years. But on 14 February, 1556, he died of a fall from his library, and after seventeen days (during which period one Mulla Bekasi appeared at The *Jharoka* in the robes of Humayun, to show the people the untruth that the Emperor was still alive), the Mughal officers read *Khutba* in the name of the 13 years old boy Emperor Jalaluddin Muhammad Akbar Padshah who later on came to be known as simply Akbar the Great.

However, it is not true to say that after the first battle of Panipat (1526), the Afghan power was totally smashed. R.P. Tripathi is quite right when he says: "Even after two brilliant victories at Panipat and on the Ghaghra, Babar could not claim to have crushed completely the Afghan power in India. Broken and demoralized though the Afghans were, the bulk of them had refused to submit to the Mughal domination. They had proclaimed Mahumd Khan Lodi their King. They were up in arms under capable and warlike leaders like Bilban, Bayazid and Maruf Farmuli, and were yet looking forward to a time when they could retrieve their honour and recover their lost sovereignty. These Afghans, when pressed hard, could find a refuge in Bihar and Bengal, and enjoyed the sympathy of the rulers of Bengal and Gujrat. It was also known that the rulers of Bengal and Gujrat were negotiating with a view to driving out the Mughals" (Tripathi, 66). The powereful Bahadur Shah of Gujrat attracted some Afghan chiefs who were driven out by the Mughals. These Afghan chiefs included Fateh Khan, Qutb Khan, Umar Khan, Alam Khan and some other Lodi nobles. They were given *Jagirs* by Bahadur Shah who was the most formidable rival of Humayun for the throne of Delhi.

So we see that ever since Babur's entry into India, the Afghans were continuously fighting, tooth and nail, against the Mughals whom they considered as foreigners and invaders, with a view to driving them out of India. These Afghans fought under the leadership of Himu, the King of Delhi, against the Mughals in the second battle of Panipat, where they capitulated, in fact for ever, to the Mughals. The Afghan-Hindu India was next to be Mughal India. The history of Northern India from the days of Ibrahim Lodi to those of Himu is the history of Afghan-Mughal conflicts for the overlordhsip of India. But below the surface of these conflicts, there was an under-current of Hindu resurgency. During his early years, Himu was a self-seeker, but since he became the Prime Minister of Adil Shah, he consciously represented the Afghan force but unconsciously represented the Hindu spirit of resurgency.

But it should be kept in mind that though the Afghans and the Mughals were at loggar-heads, yet this was but the picture of the higher-ups; in the ranks and files or in the society at large, there was the minimum of tension. Thus we find Sher Shah serving in Babur's army for fifteen months. Sher Shah also accompanied Babur in the latter's Chanderi expedition (1528) and also in the expedition to the eastern provinces (1529).

However, after Islam Shah, the Afghans continued to fight away the Mughals under the commandership of Himu, the Prime Minister of Muhammad Adil Shah (or Adili or Andhili) who clandestinely snatched away the crown from Firoze Shah, the legal successor of Islam Shah. Some historians are, probably wrong to hold the view that "The Afghan revival began with Sher Shah and almost ended with his death" (Sarkar, 1942, 47). We have, though briefly, seen how Islam Shah doggedly followed his father's parth of relentlessly fighting against the Mughal foreigners. In the next chapter we shall see how they did it under the commandership of Himu, during the reigns of Islam Shah and Adil Shah.

FAMILY TREE OF HIMU*

- Rai Jaipal Das
  - Rai Jhande Rai
    - Roop Rai
      - Naunidh Rai
      - Kewal Rai
    - Nauhind Rai
      - Mahipal Rai
        - Trilokchand Rai
        - Narain Das
        - Chaudhary Nathmal
      - Saupal Rai or Satyapal Das
  - Rai Puran Das or Puran Das *urf* Piyarao or Piparao
    - Hem Chandra or Hem Rai or Himu Shah
    - Jujhar Rao
      - ** Teharpal
      - ** Ramya

---

* According to Mr. Bhardwaj who followed Dharam Mitra's *Hemu Vir*.

** Added by this author.

CHAPTER III

Steady Rise of Himu

Himu's genealogy is probably never to be fully retrieved from the limbo. It is really to be wondered at, and regretted, as R.C. Majumdar did, that such a great and astonishing man as Himu had been was not taken cognizance of by historians, even by those that were contemporaneous with him. One reason of this is that the contemporary historians were all Muslims who were reluctant to record the exploits of an 'infidel' that Himu was. Another reason, probably, was the obscure and low heredity of Himu.

Regarding the original habitat of the family of Himu, there is a controversy between Mr. Bharadwaj and Sir Jadunath Sarkar. Mr. Bharadwaj says, "We only know that in the early medieval period, some ancestors of Hemu came from Narnaul in Haryana and settled down at a small village called Qutabpur in close proximity of Rewari" (Bharadwaj, 5). Mr. Bharadwaj's contention has the concurrence of Wolseley Haig (Haig, 1971, 71), R.C. Majumdar (Majumdar, 1984, 97) and P. Kohli (Kohli, 11). Rewari, a small town, is situated at about 28°–12' and about 76° – 38' E. It was in Mewat and was in the southern part of Alwar. Quoting from the Imperial Gazetteer of India, Mr. Bharadwaj says that Rewari was "on the Delhi-Jaipur road, thirty-two miles south west of Gurgaon, formerly a halting place on the trade road from Delhi to Rajasthan under the Mughal" (Bharadwaj, 10, f.n.). Sir Jadunath Sarkar holds a different opinion. He says that Himu or Himu Bhargav "was a Gaur Brahmin" (Sarkar, 1970, 66). The five *gotras* or clans of Brahmanas residing on the northern side of the Vindhya mountain ranges, are collectively called Pancha-Gauda. Therefore, Sir Sarkar differs from Mr. Bharadwaj on two counts. Firstly, Himu was a Brahmin and not of low caste; and secondly, the forebears of Himu moved to Delhi not from the south-west but from the south. However, no historian has given the clue to the source of his opinion.

There is another controversy regarding Himu's caste. Sir Sarkar says that he was a Brahmin (Sarkar, 1970, 66). But according to Majumdar (Majumdar, 1984, 97) and Bharadwaj (Bharadwaj, 5), Himu was a Dhunsar or Dhunsar Baniya by caste which is a "subdivision of the Vaish caste; trader, shopkeeper" (Powell-Price, *Glossary*). Bharadwaj says that "Now-a-days they (the Dhunsars – SKS) call themselves Brahmanas" (Bharadwaj, 10). Himu's *sudra* caste may have some confirmation in his profession of selling salt (but in that case he might be a *Vaishya*). Wolseley Haig says that Himu was "a Hindu of a non-fighting race" (Haig, 1971, 64). Abul Fazl says that Himu had "neither rank *(hasb)* nor race (nasab)" and that he "belonged to the Dhunsar tribe which is the lowest class of hucksters in India" (Abu-l-Fazl, 616-617). According to A.L. Basham, Himu was not a Rajput "but a pedlar by profession and a Vais'ya by caste" (Basham, 259).

"Hemu's father Puran Das (Sir Sarkar calls him Himu or Himu Bhargav – SKS) (Sarkar, 1970, 66) was a religious man and had little interest in worldly affairs. It is said that from the very childhood, he loved to live in the company of the saints and spend most of his time in meditation and singing hymns and *shabdas*. The parents did not like their son following such a course and tried to dissuade him from it. Consequently, they married him at an early age. This lady bore him two children, Basant Rai and Jujhar Rai. Basant Rai is none else but Hemu. He is also called by several other names such as Hem Raj, Hem Chandra etc." (Bharadwaj, 5-6). The religious bent of Puran Das is confirmed by the fact that, after Himu's death, when Purna Das was offered by the Mughals two extreme alternatives – acceptance of Islam or death – he chose the latter (*infra*). When Himu "had hardly progressed beyond the elementary stage of education", Puran Das "left home and went to Brindaban (Mathura) with a view to finding some *guru* who could guide him for attaining salvation. He became a disciple of a saint, Hit Harivansha, the founder of Radhavalbh sect. We know from a contemporary book '*Rasik Ananyan Mal*' by Bhagwat Mudit that Puran Das had secured for himself an enviable position among the disciples of Hit Harivansha by dint of his ability and devotion (Mr. Bharadwaj here follows Quanungo's *Sher Shah and His Times*, p. 448 – SKS). He toured from place to place preaching the ideas and ideology of the Radha Valla (sic) sect. He went as far as Thatta in Sindh. There he converted Paramanand, the Governor of that place to his sect in 1592 vik. (1535 A.D.)" (Bharadwaj, 7).

We do not know for certain when Himu was born. But we have some rough clue. Puran Das proselytised Paramanand in 1535. Before that he "secured for himself an enviable position among the disciples of Hit Harivansha" (*supra*). It might take about some four or five years to do so. Mr. Bharadwaj says that when Himu "had hardly progressed beyond the elementary stage of education (*supra*), Puran Das left home for other-worldly pursuits." It may be that Puran Das was initiated into the Radhaballav sect arround 1530, and, in that case, Himu was born around 1523 (if we take 7 as the age of beginning to learn the 3 R's). In any case Himu must have been born in the 1520s.

Himu's place of birth is also not known to us. Mr. Bharadwaj writes : "A word regarding Hemu's birth place. There is a controversy among modern writers over this question. M.L. Bhargava in his book, 'Hemu Aur Unka Yuga' (Sic), says that he was born at Deoti Macheri or Dewli Sazari (south of Delhi). In support of his contention, he quotes Abul Fazal's remark that 'after the battle of Panipat, the Mughal army went to Deoti Macheri where the residence and family of Hemu were'. This remark, as a matter of fact, does not show that Deoti Macheri was the birth place of Hemu. If it were so, Abul Fazl would have written this fact at its proper place (Mr. Bharadwaj's argument is not strong – SKS), where he describes the early life of Hemu (*Akbarnama*, vol. I, p. 617). In fact, Hemu was a rich and influential man and he could afford to build many residential palaces at different places. This does not mean that every such place was his birth place.

"Another modern writer Rahul Sankrityayana says that Hemu was born in Bihar near Sahasram (Sankrityayana is not a recognised historian – SKS). His source of information is not any contemporary or semi-contemporary book or document, but folk songs of Bihar. He observes that since women sing songs in praise of Hemu near Sahasram even to-day, he must have been born there" (Bharadwaj, 6). We can probably say that the contention of Rahul Sankrityayana bears more weight than that of Abul Fazl. Probably after his father had left hearth and home, Himu went to Deoti to seek fortune. The fact that women even to-day sing in praise of Himu has certainly some weight. But Mr. Bharadwaj writes : "Many contemporary and semi-contemporary writers like Abul Fazl, Niamatullah, etc., say that he was born at Rewari (Qutbpur). Besides, a host of noted modern historians, like K.R. Quanungo, Ishwari Prasad, V.A. Smith, Haig, etc. fully accept this view" (Bharadwaj, 7).

Himu's early education was sparingly attended to. His father remaining engrossed in religious pursuits, the responsibility of the up-bringing of Himu fell on his mother, and his grandfather, Rai Jai Pal Das. "When Hemu came of age, a Pandit and a Maulvi were employed to give him education. The former taught him Hindi, Sanskrit and elementary Arithmatic, while the latter gave him lessons in Persian and Urdu" (Bharadwaj, 7). Within a couple of years after Puran Das' departure from home, Himu's grandfather, Rai Jai Pal Das died. The family fell into hard financial constraints and so Himu had to leave school and take the profession of a huckster. At this tender age, he used to sell salt in the winding streets of Rewari.

We do not possess any authentic picture of Himu. The picture shown by Mr. Bharadwaj (after Rahul Sankrityayana) in his book *Hemu: A Critical Study of The Man and his Work* (Bharadwaj, 1), is perhaps not trustworthy because he does not mention the provenance of it. Moreover, the picture shows Himu with a *modestly beautiful mien riding on horse-back, wearing a sword*, which is contradicted by Abul Fazal and William Erskine. Abul Fazl says that Himu had no "beauty of form (*surat*) nor noble qualities (*sairat*)" (*infra*) and was "*evil-looking one of puny form*" (Abul-l-Fazl, 616-167). Himu's having a puny physique is attested by V.A. Smith (Smith, 26). Erskine also says that Himu's "frame was so feeble that he could not ride on horse-back, and even in the field was forced to be carried about in a litter or on an elephant" (*infra*) and that Himu was of a "mean deportment, hard favoured, and of low stature" (*infra*) and that he "*never wore a sword*" (emphases added) (Erskine, 490 f.n.).

Finding the family financially constrained, Himu at a very tender age, began to sell saltpetre (according to Abul Fazl) or became a "green-grocer" (according to Majumdar) (S.C. Sarkar, 7) or simply a "shopkeeper" (*bakkal*) (according to P. Kohli) or a seller of "worthless wares" (according to Erskine) (Erskine, 490). We do not know how Himu drew the sympathetic sight of Islam Shah. But it may be that "By sheer dint of hard work and honesty of purpose, he became a *Chaudhury* (respectable person – SKS) in his own circle. This brought him into contact with the Government officials who introduced him into the Court of the Sultan" (Mahajan, 57). Abul

Fazl writes that Himu "by means of astuteness" became a government huckster (Abu-l-Fazl, 617) and by "masterpieces of feline trickery he gradually made himself known to Salim Khan by evil-speaking and *business capacity*" (italics mine) (*ibid.*). It may be noted here that though Abul Fazl used vituperation against Himu, he, unawares, admitted Himu's "business capacity" and, as we shall see later on, Islam's selection of Himu proved fortuitous. Frederick Augustus also says that Himu "was a man of no ordinary character" (Augustus, 72); Sir Sarkar speaks of his "conspicuous ability for war and civil administration alike" (Sarkar, Sir, 66); and H.G. Rawlinson says that Himu was "clever" (Rawlinson, 174). Therefore, it seems that Abul Fazl is unjust when he writes that "Perchance the incomparable Deity raised him (Himu – SKS) to high position (under Islam Shah – SKS) for some occult reason which was hidden from the eyes of the acute, or perhaps He sent one worse than themselves to chastise the wicked of the eye" (Abu-l-Fazl, 617). Himu certainly captivated the attention of Islam Shah with his native and inordinate qualities.

It was even during the time of Islam Shah that Himu climbed high up the ladder of royal favours. Islam Shah made him *Shahana* or Superintendent of Delhi market. But, according to *Tarikh-i-Sultan-i-Afghana* of Ahmed Yadgar, Himu was a "weighman in the *bazar*" (Dowson, 1955, 69). Perhaps the designations "Superintendent" and "Weighman" were synonymous for all practical purposes. Here also Abul Fazl holds a different opinion. He says that Himu was a "Government huckster under Salim Khan" (Abu-l-Fazl, 617). But according to *Kholaset ul Tawarikh*, Himu "was made Modi-e-Sirkar, an office, probably, nearly corresponding to that of purveyor" (Erskine, 490 f.n.). May be, Himu was at first government huckster and then elevated to the higher position of Superintendent (*Shahana*).

However, very soon Himu was promoted by Islam Shah to the rank of *Daroga-i-Chauki* or the head of Department of Intelligence and Posts. All these rapid promotions prove beyond doubt that Himu was intelligent and trustworthy, and that he had outstanding administrative capacity. Islam continued to bestow laurels upon Himu, but yet high administrative and military duties were not charged of him. He was vested with high administrative and military powers only during the reign of Muhammad Adil Shah.

Between Islam Shah who died in November, 1554, and Muhammad Adil Shah, there was only three days' reign of Firuz Shah, yet it was full of activities, for "Coins was struck, and the prayer for the reigning prince (Firuz – SKS) offered, in his name" (Erskine, 483). As Firuz was very young, the state business was run by Taj Khan who "issued whatever orders he chose" (Dowson, 1955, 63). The nobles were disgruntled at this and remonstrated before Bibi Bai (mother of Firuz) who sent Taj Khan to Malwa, as a redressing measure. But on the third day of the unfortunate child-sovereign's reign, Mubariz Khan, his uncle, with an open sword "entered the private apartments of the palace with the intention of putting to death the Young King" (Erskine, 483 f.n.) "feigning eccentricity and madness, in order to escape death or blinding" (Dowson, 1955, 64), with a band of armed musclemen. It may be noted here that according to Elliot, the rueful incident perhaps occurred within a week of Firuz's reign : "According to others, this murder occurs within a week (three days being the general statement)" (Dowson, 1955, 65 note). However, Firuz's mother Bibi Bai, variously called Bibi Banu, Bibi Bhi and Bibi Mahi (according to Erskine, the last one is a mistake), on perceiving the immediate danger, cried out at the top of her voice and rushed to stop Mubariz and "seizing the hem of his robe, with prayers and tears besought him spare his sister's boy; offering to convey the youth to some far distant land where he would live as a private person, and never aspire to be King; or, if that was not allowed her, she prayed her brother at least to spare her son's life, though doomed to imprisonment, however severe. But Mobarez (Mobariz Khan – SKS), throwing her off, seized" the Young King, and barbarously murdered him in his mother's arms" (Erskine, 483). The murder of Firuz was possible partially due to the extreme fidelity of Bibi Bai in her brother, Mubariz Khan. We know that Islam Shah, when he was terminally ill, conspired to eliminate all those that might come in the way of his son's ascension to the throne. Islam Shah "had formed the most unfavourable opinion of Mobariz Khan, and feared his attempts on the life of his son, had repeately resolved to put him to death, and was as often prevented only by her (Bibi Bai's – SKS) intervention and tears. After he had taken to his death-bed, the King again told Bibi Bai that she must chose between her brother and her son; that if she valued her son's life, she must suffer her brother to be taken out of the way ; that there was no other security for the prince. But Bibi Bai, who thought Islam's suspicions unfounded, and that Mobariz was too much of a voluptuary, and too much devoted to idle amusement to be ambitious, finally prevailed upon her husband to spare the future murderer of their son" (Erskine, 484). In fact, even during the active life of Islam Shah, Mubariz hatched a conspiracy against him: "A conspiracy was hatched against Islam Shah and preparations were made in secret. There was a revolt in which Adil and many other Afghan nobles took part. The revolt was a failure as some of the details were miscarried. Khawas Khan was defeated. He ran away as a rebel. Adil also disappeared for ever" (Mahajan, 1964, 51). Bibi Bai or Bibi Banu or Bibi Mahi was right in holding Mubariz a out-of-the-run non-desecript sensualist, or Wolseley Haig says that Mubariz "simulated imbecility, probably without much effort, for he was certainly of the defective intellect. He devoted his time almost entirely to frivolous and sensual pleasure and was contemtuously known as Adli (the Afghans called him Andhli or the blind and the Hindus called him Adili or the fool – SKS) which is a contemptuous diminutive of his title" (Haig, 1971, 64-65).

Here, perhaps, we might hazard some comments. Mubariz, though allegedly imbecile, might have animus against Islam Shah. It is true that after Sher Shah, his eldest son Adil Khan had the pre-emptive right to the throne, according to the ancient and prevailing law of primogeniture. In fact, Adil Khan fought for the throne, but, as he was weak in fibre, he ultimately gave way to Islam. So, Mubariz might have taken Islam to be an usurper, and really this act of Islam was an "act of perfidy towards his brother" (Waley, 252). And this is clear from the fact that at the time of Sher Shah's death, Adil Khan, the eldest son of Sher Shah, was at Ranathombore, a place far away from Kalinjar. But the younger son, Jalal Khan (the future Islam Shah – SKS), who was near the capital, "being favoured by a strong party of the principal Amirs, arrived in the camp in three days. There, chiefly through the influence of Isa Khan Hijab, he was proclaimed King ..." (Erskine, 448). The "ostensible reason" (*ibid.*) given out by the Amirs was that Adil Khan "was of a depraved character" (*ibid.*) and that the premonition of a rebellion necessitated such a prompt decision. We may probably offer at least two arguments in favour of this contention. Firstly, even during the life-time of Islam, Mubariz attempted murder on Islam. Secondly, immediately after ascension, Mubariz assumed the title of Adil Shah, which event might have some nostalgic touch, because the name of Islam's elder brother was also Adil.

Firuz's murder was precipitated by another fact. As Firuz was too young. One Taj Khan Kirani (or Karrani), the *wazir*, acted as his agent. This Taj Khan was not interested in, and did not care for, the affairs of the state "and issued whatever orders he chose" (*infra*), which fact disaffected a sizable number of nobles who led a remonstrance to Bibi Bai. The lady immediately sent Taj Khan, to whom Islam Shah "consigned the boy (Firuz – SKS) to his care" (*infra*), to Malwa. "About *a month* after Taj Khan's departure, Mamrez Khan (Mubariz Khan – SKS), her (Bibi Bai's – SKS) brother, son of Mian Nizam (Nizam Khan – SKS), brother of Sher Shah (who had lived at Bayana, feigning eccentricity and madness, in order to escape death or blinding under the late reign), thought this a good opportunity of offering his congratulations to his nephew, and, under the pretence, of making away with him and seizing the crown for himself .... So after *two months*, he entered Gwalior with a large army, and, all covered with dust as he was, went direct into the presence of Firuz Khan, with the intention of seizing and expelling him" (italics mine) (Dowson, 1955, 63-64). It may be pointed out here that historians are not unanimous on the length of Firuz's reign; some say three days; some a week; and some a month or two months – "three days being the general statement" (Dowson, 64).

"Seven days after the slaughter of Firuz Khan, Mamrez (Elliot always calls Mubariz Mamrez – SKS) Khan came to the throne. Before he took possession of it, he caused tents of damask and brocade to be erected in the *bazar*; after which, he seated himself on the throne and assumed the title of' Adil Shah." (Dowson, 65) (There was an Adil Khan I or Adil Shah who ruled Khandesh from 1441 to 1457 when he died). But "Waki' at-i Mushlaki says he (Adil Shah – SKS) was raised to the throne with the title of Sultan Mahmud" (Dowson, 1955, 65 f.n.). However, Adil then showered so much of elaborate titles and fisc-drying largesse on the nobles, that "after two months, he found that every one was well inclined towards him" (Dowson, 1955, 66) and made Chunar (near modern Benares – SKS) his residential capital. Earlier, the Afghan capital was in Gwalior, and now probably both Gwalior and Chunar were his capitals, or perhaps only the latter one.

Here a few lines about Adil's character may not be out of place, because it was this his unbecoming strangeness that contributed much to the high-rise of Himu. Kashim Ferista writes that "Adily having always devoted himself to pleasure, neglected even the common acquirements of reading and writing. He hated men of learning, and kept company with illiterate persons like himself, whom he raised to the highest dignities in the state, ..." (Ferista, 89). He would spend "his time in excess among the inmates of his harem" (*ibid.*) and would open the treasury at his whims to men of any rank.

Adil was very original (in the French sense of the term) and notorious for his exemplary indulgence in foppery and spendthriftiness and debauchery (incidentally "आदिल" means "righteous"), with only one saving grace of having a good taste, like Baj Bahadur after him, for music and dance, whence his epithet "Adil" or "Andhali". "In the text of the *Tarikh-i-Daudi* it is Andhali meaning "blind'. Perhaps the common people gave him this nickname because of his dissolute and senseless ways. Abul Fazl writes "Adali which Beveridge translates by 'tyrant'. Dorn writes 'Adali and says it means 'foolish'." (Prasad, 190 f.n.). But the connoisseur wasted himself even in these arts with overindulgence. Adil loved low companion and shameless flattery. When he heard of the height of the magnificence and generosity of Sultan Mohammad Tughluq, he grew a passion to excell it and accordingly opened several times the lock of his treasury and drained it dry. He would, as is recorded in *Makhzan-i-Afghani* and *Tarikh-i-Daudi* and other such works, on occasions parade through streets with a long train behind, shooting golden-headed arrows; as per the royal regulation, one who could retrieve such an arrow, would be rewarded with a sum of five hundred *tangas* (about £ 200, to-day) in money.

However, on his accession he raised a number of officers of the lower rungs to high positions. He appointed Shamshir Khan the *wazir* and lieutenant of the palace. Shamshir, the brother of the celebrated Khawas Khan, was a slave of Sher Shah. Adil also raised Doulat Khan Nouhani to the higher rank with the charge of the Nouhanis. Thus, "Himu Bakkal, a Hindu, was raised to offices of high trust, and soon became the minister who exercised the most commanding authority." (Erskine, 486). As is admitted by every one, Himu was man of efficiency *par excellence*. He was, as if, a factotum in the reign of Adil. So the charge against Adil that he bestowed inordinate favour on only Himu is unfounded. Nevertheless, all these moves of Adil gave a fillip to the seething discontent among the Afghans.

A palace incidence, almost immediately after Adil's ascension, is of some importance. It betrays the weakness of the internal administration. Adil, who would not appear at the Court often, one day was busy at the Court distributing *jagirs*. The *jagir* of Kanauj had been held by Muhammad Farmuli. Adil snatched it away from him and conferred it on Sirmast Khan Sirpani who was also an Afghan though of a low rank. Firmuli's son, Sikandar Khan, was already unhappy with the Afghan administration because once Sher Shah wanted to kill, but instead put behind the bars, his father Firmuli. So salt was added to the wound when Adil snatched his father's *jagir* to give it to Sirmast Khan, and he arrogantly opposed such a transfer in the open Court in a foul language. Confusion prevailed in the *Darbar*. Sirmast tried to pacify Sikandar Khan and thus make him a prisoner. Perceiving the trick of Sirmast, Sikandar whisked a dagger and plunged it deep in the chest of Sirmast who dropped dead. The nobles ran helter-skelter while the King ensconced himself in the harem. Within moments, Ibrahim Khan Sur, the husband of Adil's sister, overpowered Sikandar with the help of some nobles and put him to death. Incidentally, within one month after his ascension, Adil moved against the Raja of Andrum. Here, H.M. Elliot narrates a very curious event following what Adil "beheld in a dream" (Dowson, 1955, 67 68).

While Adil had been passing through such trying circumstances, Himu was gradually climbing up the ladder of administrative hierarchy. We may surmise that this was possible because, finding himself in a tense regard of high suspicion, Adil selected a Hindu – because Hindus were more dependable, more so, probably, because they had less muscle-power – as an officer, who had by then already proved his honesty and worth, for a high position in the army. Historians say that Himu fought as many as twentytwo battles, before he fought the 2nd battle of Panipat, and in each one he came out successful. But, unfortunately, historians have not narrated all the twentytwo battles of Himu. Perhaps some of these "battles" were mere skirmishes and so escaped the notice of historiographers. However, we have collected from different sources the narratives of as many battles as are available. Further researches about the unknown battles will certainly be welcome.

Himu's rise was not sudden but gradual and steady. During the time of Islam Shah, Himu could not rise above the position of the Superintendent of Bazars (Sheikhji Bazar). Adil being indulgent, worthless and inexperienced, and being apathetic to the "drudgery of business, handed over to Himu all the important portfolios of the state and thus raised him to the highest rank of the Prime Minister and "generalissimo" (Sarkar and Datta, 7), and himself became only a symbol of the state. Himu became so powerful that he distributed *jagirs* at his will, and "got possession of the royal elephants, as well as of the treasures which had been accumulated by the last two Kings, and he freely expended what they had collected" (Erskine, 492). Nevertheless, William Erskine is of the opinion that the choice of Himu as the Prime Minister was a sound one on the part of Adil. But this was not an unmixed blessing to Himu, because it "naturally created him enemies among the Afghan chiefs, who having conspired against his life, revolted from his authority" (Ferista, 89).

Himu had the opportunity of showing his skill and mettle in the battle-fields owing to the spate of rebellions that occurred soon after Adil's capture of the throne. Taj Khan Karrani, to whom Islam Shah consigned Firuz to take care of the boy, and whom Bibi Bai, Islam's wife, sent to Malwa (*supra*) was the first to raise the standard of rebellion. Next to do so was Ibrahim Khan Sur, husband of Adil's sister. Ibrahim Sur captured Delhi and Agra and proclaimed himself independent. Ahmed Khan Sur, the husband of another sister of Adil and governor of Lahore, also did not sit idle but proclaimed his independence and withal assumed the title of Sikandar Shah.

In the eastern portion of the Empire also rebellion broke out. Muhammad Khan Sur, the governor of Bengal, assumed the title of Samsuddin Muhammad Shah Ghazi and began to rule independently. So we find that the Sur Empire left by Islam Shah broke into four principal pieces: (i) Delhi and Agra became independent under Ibrahim Shah; (ii) Punjab became independent under Sikandar Shah; (iii) Bengal became independent under Samsuddin Muhammad Shah Ghazi; and (iv) Only the stretch of land from Agra to Bihar remained under the suzerainty of Adil.

To add to the unlucky days of the Sur Empire, some chiefs and nobles also revolted. For example, Ghazi Khan Sur of Bayana, Hazi Khan of Alwar and Yahya Turan of Shamba, each one of them, tried to grab as much portion of the Empire as they could and thus brought the Empire to a point of dissolution. It may be pointed out here that had not there been such inordinate internecine struggle for vested interests within the Sur Empire, the Mughals might not, till the time of Himu, have made a dent in it. And it certainly goes to the credit of Himu that he could tide over the high-rise surges in the Sur Empire.

II

So far we have known only of eleven military exploits out of the supposed twentytwo battles that Himu is said to have accomplished. These are being briefly narrated under :

(i) The First Battle of Himu

Perceiving the weakness of Adil Shah, Junaid Khan, the governor of Bayana, with the help of Foujdar of Ajmer, devasted Ajmer. To punish the culprits, Adil detached Jamal Khan from Chunar. A battle took place at Kanulupur near Ladnah in which Jamal Khan was routed. No sooner had the tiding reached Adil than he sent heavy reinforcements under Himu, the Commander-in-Chief. Junaid Khan also sent an army under Daulat Khan. On the night before the battle Himu mustered the soldiery around him and delivered an inspiring oration for victory. The soldiers being moved pounched upon the armoury of Daulat Khan at day-break and slew Daulat Khan, the Commander, whose army took to heels. Himu pursued them upto two *Kos* and made short works with many of them.

(ii) The Second Battle of Himu

Junaid Khan did not want to eat his humble pie, and so marched against Himu with 8,000 cavalry, 3,000 foot, and a number of elephants, and a large park of artillery. Junaid's army far exceeded that of Himu in strength. Himu had only 3,000 horses and so he thought of the worst. Frontal fighting might be self-defeating, and so Himu decided upon pre-emptive night attack. For three watches of the night, Junaid's soldiery remained awake, but in the small hours of the night they fell asleep, when Himu made a lightning attack. The unprepared soldiers were not allowed even the time to dress up and most of them succumbed to the hacking of Himu's soldiers. Even, in the thick darkness of the night, Junaid's soldiers were slaughtering themselves.

(iii) The Third Battle of Himu

This time Himu fought with Taj Khan Karrani. Perceiving the weakness of the administration of Adil Shah, Taj Khan Karrani, brother of Sulaiman Karrani, came out of Gwalior and rushed towards Bengal with the alleged intention of ruling over Bengal, independently. Getting this tiding, Adil sent a strong flying column which engaged Taj Khan in a battle at Chibra-Mow or Chhatramau (about forty *Kos* from agra and thirty from Kanauj) and defeated him. Taj Khan, effecting his escape, proceeded towards Chunar. On the way, he "took possession of several local treasures belonging to 'Adil, and enriched himself with their contents. He also seized a troop (*halka*) of elephants, one hundred in number, and went and joined his brother 'Imad, Sulaiman and Khwaja I'lyas, who held several districts on the banks of the Ganges and at Khawaspur Tanda" (Dowson, 242-43). Adil now moved from Gwalior to Chunar to Chastise the Kararanis. The two armies met on the opposite banks of the Ganges, without any engagment. "At last Hemu, who was now high in the King's confidence made a proposal, that if he were allowed to take a few elephants, he would undertake to cross the river, to attack the enemy, and to destroy them. The King having led his troops over the river, engaged the Kararanis in a battle, which, though desperately contested, ended in a complete victory" (Erskine, 489-90).

(iv) The Fourth Battle of Himu

Though the rebellion of the Karranis was suppressed by Himu, yet further rebellions broke out everywhere. The governors of the provinces were very much powerful with standing armies under their command. Adil's suspicious disposition and unpredictable moves gave a fillip to the rebellious motives of the governors. Thus Ibrahim Khan Sur who was with the charge of Chunar (near modern Benaras) fled to the protection of his father Ghazi Khan, the governor of Biana and Hindaun. The irrate Adil despatched Isa Khan Niyazi in pursuit of Ibrahim. The two armies of Niyazi and of Ibrahim met near Kalpi on the bank of the Ganges, about 200 miles east of Agra, and an action took place in which Ibrahim defeated Isa Khan. Ibrahim now openly threw off his allegiance to Adil, marched towards Delhi and Agra, occupied both the places, and ascended the throne of Delhi. On receipt of this alarming news, Adil temporarily put off his design of punishing the Kararanis (or Karranis) and proceeded from Chunar towards Delhi. Ibrahim met him on the way and submitted; but soon changed mind when some Afghan nobles joined issue with him. Adil retreated to Chunar via Panna, leaving Ibrahim the Sultan of Agra, Delhi and the neighbouring provinces of Hindustan.

Of the three other main splinter provinces of Adil's empire, the Punjab, was under Ahmed Khan Sur, cousin of Sher Shah and husband of Adil's sister, assumed the title of Sultan Sikandar Shah. The three provinces of the Punjab, Malwa and Bengal were quarrelling with each other to carve out a portion of the neighbour. Malwa was under Shiya or Sazawal Khan and Bengal was a bone of contention between Sultan Muhammad Shah Sur and Taj Khan Kararani. Besides, Tatar Khan Kasi, Haibat Khan and Nasib Khan Taghuchi, all of whom served under Islam Shah, hated Adil. Taking this opportunity, Sikandar Shah, with the help of these rebels marched towards Delhi and Agra, at the head of ten or twelve thousand horses. Sultan Ibrahim, who just before this once submitted to Adil but later changed his mind, also moved westwards, after profuse distribution of *Kanats* (screens), *Alem*, *Tugh*, *nakara*, etc. among nobles and the lower files, for boosting up morale. A battle ensued at Farra and, Ibrahim being defeated, Sikandar occupied Delhi and Agra.

In order to legalise his occupation of the throne of Delhi, Sikandar threw a grand banquet before the nobles, to buy their support, in which he delivered a demagogic speech. He reminded the assembly that "their implacable enemy Humayun, who had now conquered Kabul and had no longer any brothers who could thwart design, was ready to pour down upon them with the whole force of his dominions, and to reap the fruit of their infatuations; that the only hope of the Afghans lay in union; that if they consented to lay aside private feuds and act in concert like a band of brothers, they could still *repel the son of Baber*; that their interest was that .... The assembly, with one voice, called out the Sikandar Shah (sic), the worthy cousin of Sher Shah, was the wished-for person, and that he alone should be their leader and sovereign" (italics mine) (Erskine, 497-98).

Sikandar was now preparing himself to mount an attack upon Adil with a view to carrying out Bihar and Bengal from the latter, but then the unsavoury news arrived that Humayun, capturing Kabul, had been contemplating on an attack on the Punjab. Sikandar forthwith detached forty thousand horse under Tatar Khan and Haibat Khan, but Bairam Khan, on the side of Humayun, defeated the two generals at Machiwara on the bank of the Sutlej (some thirty miles north-west of modern Chandigarh). Both Sikandar and Humayun sent reinforcements. In the end Sikandar gave way and ensconced himself in the Sewalik mountains. He attempted a retribution, but had to repair to Bengal where he seized the reign of government only to die soon.

(v) The Fifth Battle of Himu

Himu fought with Ibrahim Khan Sur thrice and thrice defeated him. When Sikandar had been proceeding towards the Punjab, Sultan Ibrahim Khan Sur came out of his retreat in Sambal, crossed the Ganges and marched towards Kalpi (near and opposite modern Rai Bareli), in order to retrieve his Kingdom. At the same time Adil sent Himu, then the Prime Minister, from Chunar at the head of a big army, to occupy Agra and Delhi, left behind by Sikandar (the throne of Delhi during this time had virtually been vacant). Himu met Ibrahim at Kalpi. Ibrahim had collected a large army consisting of Afghans, Nouhanis and the men of the zamindars of Biana, and thus armed, attacked Himu who gave Ibrahim a crushing defeat. Ibrahim ensconced himself in the fastness of Khanwa. Himu followed him and beseiged the fortress.

(vi) The Sixth Battle of Himu

Being short of victuals, Ibrahim appealed to his father who supplied provisions to the fortress at Khanwa through the neighbouring hills. His father helped him also with reinforcements. Thus, receiving appui from his father, Ibrahim again engaged himself in a battle with Himu and again was vanquished by him.

(vii) The Seventh Battle of Himu

Meantime, Sikandar Khan revolted in Bengal, adding a new trouble to the trouble-torn empire of Adil. The half-broken Ibrahim found in this a golden opportunity for measuring swords with Himu, and so drew his army at the village of Mandakar, six miles from Agra. A battle ensued and Ibrahim was for the third and last time defeated by Himu.

(viii) The Eighth Battle of Himu

While Himu, thus, was engaged in the western theatre, rebellion broke out in the eastern province of Bengal where its governor, Muhammad Khan Sur, "a near relation of Sher Shah" (Erskine, 500), took the title of Sultan Jalal-ud-din, and declared himself independent and advanced towards Bihar to occupy it as well as Jaunpur and Delhi. Perceiving this new danger in his Kingdom, Adil, losing no time, recalled Himu from the seige of Khanwa, though Himu had been battering the fortress for three months then. Himu forthwith abandoned the seige and proceeded to report to Adil, but Sultan Ibrahim Sur attacked him near the village Mandhakar and was himself decidedly defeated. Ibrahim fled to the protection of Haji Khan in Alwar. Himu "detached his nephew with a strong force, who pursued the flying prince for two or three stages, and then returned" (Erskine, 500).

(ix) The Ninth Battle of Himu

After the defeat of Sultan Ibrahim at Mandhakar, Himu marched down the Jumna with lightning speed and joined Adil. We have earlier seen that Adil had been proceeding towards Bengal to punish Muhammad Shah Sur who took the title of Jalal-ud-din and who conspired to extend his country upto Jaunpur. Jalal-ud-din's army had by then already reached Jaunpur and the King himself reached Chaperghata (or Chhapar Mau), about 30 miles from Kalpi. Here the two armies met on the opposing banks of Jumna. The army of Jalal-ud-din was highly equipped and so the Sultan expected natural victory. "But the sudden and unexpected arrival of Himu changed the face of affairs. The moment he came, he sent his troops across, and fording the river with his elephants, fell on the army of Bengal by surprise. The resistance made was comparatively trifling. The enemy (Jalal's army – SKS), in the obscurity of night, could distinguish nothing, and forsook their camp. The slaughter was great among the fugitives. Many Amirs of rank perished ...... Muhammad (Jalal-ul-din Khan Sur – SKS) himself was never heard of more .... the whole camp, and the property that it contained, became the prey of the conquerors" (Erskine, 503).

But Sir Jadunath Sarkar here differs from Erskine. According to him Muhammad Khan declared independence of Bengal and took the title of Samsuddin Muhammad Shah Ghazi, "raided Arracan, occupied Jaunpur and advanced towards Agra, but was slain by the royal general Himu at Chhaparghat (Chhapar Mau) 30 miles east of Kalpi, c. December, 1555. After this victory 'Adili appointed Shahbaz Khan as his governor of Bengal. But Shamsuddin's son Khizr Khan immediately after his father's death crowned himself at Jhusi (opposite Allahabad), took the title of Ghiyasud-din Bahadur Shah, and later in the year (1556) invaded Bengal overcoming Shahabaz Khan and making himself master of that province" (Sir Sarkar, 1977, 179).

(x) The Tenth Battle of Himu

After the battle of Chhaparghata, the two great contestants for the throne of Chunar, Sultan Ibrahim Sur and Muhammad Khan Sur (Jalal-ud-din), were wiped off by Adil with the able generalship of Himu. Meanwhile, Humayun, the Mughal emperor, after his victory over Sikandar Shah at Sirhind, occupied Delhi and Agra, but soon after this died of a fall from his library on 23rd July, 1555. Humayun's young son, the 13 years old Akbar and his regent Bairam Khan were then at Jullundur, in the Punjab, about 200 miles away from Delhi. The death of Humayun was kept a secret for seventeen days, Mulla Bekasi appearing at the regular *Jharoka* with the late emperor's insignia (Sher Shah's death was kept secret for five days, and Jhala Ajja acted as a proxy of Rana Sanga in the battle of Khanwa). At the news of Humayun's death a great hope grew in Adil's heart. He thought of wiping out the Mughals off Hindustan. With this end in view, Adil flew to Chunar in order to raise a great army, and withal detached Himu with "an army of fifty thousand horses and five hundred elephants towards Agra, to take advantage of this occurrence (death of Humayun – SKS), to recover what had been lost, and *to expel invaders from his Kingdom*" (Italics mine) (Erskine, 503). Meantime, Akbar was proclaimed Emperor.

When Himu's army reached the outskirts of Agra, "Sekander Khan Uzbek and the other generals of Emperor Akbar, who had succeeded his father, sensible that they were unable to resist so powerful a force, retreated to Delhi. Himu, having occupied Agra, pursued the retreating enemy" (Erskine,, 503), upto Tughlaqabad, a village about 5 miles east of the Qutb Minar. Here Tardi Beg Khan, the Mughal governor of Delhi, gave Himu a battle on 7th October, 1556. Himu had 1,000 elephants, 50,000 horses, 51 cannons and 500 falconates – an army of beings, writes Ferista, " 'as numerous as the locusts and ants of the deserts' " (Kohli, 12). Sir Jadunath Sarkar has given a graphic description of the course of the battle : "The Mughal army was thus drawn up: Abdullah Uzbeg commanded the van, Haidar Muhammad the right wing, Iskandar Beg the left, and Tardi Beg himself the centre. The choice Turki cavalry in the van and left wing attacked and drove back the enemy forces before them; and followed for in pursuit. In this assault the victors captured 400 elephants and slew 3,000 men of the Afghan army. Imagining victory already gained, many of Tardi Beg's followers dispersed to plunder the enemy camp, and he was left in the field very thinly guarded. All

EMPERORS ON THE THRONE OF DELHI

BAHLUL LODI (1451 - 1489)

|

SIKANDAR LODI (1489 - 1517)
(Capital transferred to Agra)

|

IBRAHIM LODI (1517 - 1526)
(Capital Transferred to Delhi)

|

BABUR (1526 - 1530)

|

HUMAYUN (1530 - 1539/ Battle of Chausa)

.
.
.

HUMAYUN (1555 - 1556)

|

*HIMU (1556)

|

AKBAR (1556 - 1605)

---

* Added by this author

this time Himu had been holding 300 choice elephants and a force of select horsemen as a reserve in the centre. He promptly seized the opportunity and made a sudden charge upon Tardi Beg with his reserve. At the impetuous advance of the huge beasts and the dense cavalry behind them, many of the Mughal officers fled away in terror without waiting to offer a fefense. At last Tardi Beg himself took the same course (Tardi Beg should not have left himself unguarded and allowed the officers to disperse and loot enemy property. Himu, later on, himself committed this blunder in the second battle of Panipat – SKS)" (Sarkar, Sir, 1970, 67). Tardi Beg, straight from the battle ground, proceeded towards the Punjab, and Himu forthwith occupied Delhi." Himu was so elated by his victories and by the capture of Delhi as to believe that he had already reached the goal of his ambition. He made no pretence of restoring his master, but *assumed the title of Raja Vikramaditya and is said to have struck coins bearing his titles*, though no specimen is known to exist" (italics mine) (Haig, 1971, 72). Himu's next object was "to supplement the occupation of Delhi by the conquest of the Punjab" (Hunter, 1986, 67).

There is a controversy among historians regarding whether, after his occupation of the throne of Delhi, Himu acted as a representative of Adil, or he became an independent King. Circumstantial evidences prove beyond doubt that he became an independent King of Delhi. We have just now noticed that according to Haig, Himu became an independent King, on all counts. According to Sarkar and Datta, Himu assumed the title of *Vikramaditya* or *Vikramadity* (Sarkar and Datta, 56). But Michael Edwardes writes that Himu "declared himself King under the title of Raja Vikramaditya" (Edwardes, 139). Himu's proclamation of his being a Raja is very significant. The title of Raja reminds one of the ancient and medieval Indian Hindu Kings. Had there been no intention of Himu to become an independent King, he would not have borne the title of Raja. In fact, Himu was reminiscent of the past glory of the Hindus. However, R.C. Majumdar is also of the opinion that Himu "assumed independence, with the title of Raja Vikramaditya" (Majumdar, 1984, 96).

The assumption of the "historic" (Majumdar) name of Vikramaditya is also significant as it may innuendo the Hindu mentality (of revival) of Himu. Himu might have been nursing in the inner regard of his heart the image of King Vikramaditya of Ujjain (c. 56 B.C.); or Himu might have in his mind the name of the founder of Delhi – the "Hindu King called Biguer Magid (Bikramjit) by whom the name of Delhi was given to it (the meaning of the word "Dehli" is "steadfast"– SKS)" (Manucci, 108).

However, J.C. Powell-Price says that Himu "was not intending to win Delhi for the Suri dynasty but for himself" (Powell-Price, 246). W.H. Moreland and Sir. A.C. Chatterjee also say that "disregarding his absent master, he (Himu – SKS) assumed the throne for himself" (Moreland, 215). According to *The New Encyclopaedia Britannica*, 1981, 'Hemu, a Hindu minister (of Adil – SKS) claimed (the throne of Delhi – SKS) for himself' (Ency. Brit. vol. I, 400). Ishwari Prasad is confident that Himu hoped to rule over Hindustan: "Humayun's sudden death, aided by the circumstance that his son was a mere lad of 13, revived Hemu's hopes of securing the Empire of Hindustan" (Prasad, 228). Ishwari Prasad continues : "Master of Delhi and Agra, Hemu set his forces in order and made a bold bid for the Empire of Hindustan" (*ibid.*). V.A. Smith thinks that Himu "was inspired by the idea of founding a Hindu *raj*" (*infra*) and thought it "better to gain a Kingdom for his own benefit rather than for that of his absent employer" (*infra*) and that this "is supported by his assumption of the title Vikramaditya" (Majumdar, 1984, 100). R.C. Majumdar says that Himu "wistfully looked towards the sovereignty of Hindustan" (*ibid.*). It may be that it was with this end in view that Himu once "sowed dissension between the King (Adil – SKS) and his leading nobles" (Haig, 1971, 65). Sir Wolseley Haig is quite correct when he writes that throughout his career, Himu "was preparing to expel the Mughals from India, nominally in the interest of 'Adil, but actually in his own. Himu secretly cherished designs of seizing for himself the imperial throne (of Delhi – SKS) and restoring the dominion to the Hindus" (*italics mine*) (Haig, 1971, 71). Finding the imbecility of Adil, Himu might have such a design, but, probably, he could not nurse such a design before he became the Commander-in-Chief of Adil. Lt. Col. H.C. Kar is very clear on this point. He says, "After taking the capital Hemu came to the conclusion that he had better claim the throne for himself rather on behalf of Abdali (Adil – SKS). He assumed the title of Vikramaditya. He emerged as a monarch in his own right, *the only Hindu to occupy the throne of Delhi during the medieval history of India*" (italics mine) (Kar, 283).

Whether Himu struck coins bearing his title is of less significance, as it can never be a negative evidence of his claiming the throne for himself, because we are not in the possession of all the historical finds. But, R.C. Majumdar writes that Himu "issued coins in his name" (*infra*) and that he occupied Delhi with the concurrence of the Afghans; and "declared his independent status in a practical manner by ascending the throne, with the imperial canopy raised over his head" (Majumdar, 1984, 100). To buy the support of the Afghans for his ascension, assumption of the title of Vikramaditya and all that, Himu resorted to the liberal distribution of largesse. On the other hand, he sent nominal allegiance to Adil and thus "concealed his usurpation, and pretended to be acting in his master's name" (Smith, 28). Stanley Walpert concurs. He says that Himu had been "seeking to restore Hindu power. He seized both cities (of Delhi and Agra – SKS) and proclaimed himself Raja Vikramaditya ('King whose Effulgence is Equal to the Sun's')" (Walpert, 126). Bamber Gascoigne also says that "Hemu then entered Delhi and set himself up as an independent ruler under the Hindu title of Vikramaditya" (Gascoigne, 71). Himu's independence of Adil is supported also by the fact that after his ascension, before whatever move he took, he did not seek any permission from, or concurrence of, Adil. Therefore, we may probably conclude that the opinion of R.C. Majumdar is subdued when he calls Himu a "Hindu Hero" and not a Hindu King of Delhi.

There may be controversy regarding whether Himu's ascending the throne of Delhi and declaring himself independent is morally justifiable or not. On this point one should not, perhaps, be an extreme moralist like Cato, for historical morality or morality in history is not time-independent. Himu's action was not strange; it was the go of the day. So, R.C. Majumdar is quite right when he writes: "But a little reflection will show that there was nothing unreasonable or immoral in the aspiration of Himu" (Majumdar, 1984, 100). Further, as Adil was "certainly of defective intellect" (Haig, 1971, 65), it was rather morally obligatory, to some extent, on the part of Himu, to shoulder the burden of the kingdom, albeit under his own insignia.

However, Himu ruled independently from the throne of Delhi for only thirty days (from 7th October, 1556, on which he won the battle of Tughlaqabad and captured Delhi, to 5th November, 1556, on which he lost the second battle of Panipat and shed his last drop of blood before Akbar).

CHAPTER IV

The Second Battle of Panipat, Accidental Death of Himu, and the Consequences Thereof

A

When the battle of Tughlaqabad was going on "The Emperor (Akbar – SKS) and his followers were engaged at Jalandhar in counteracting the effects of Sultan Ibrahim" (Dowson, 1964, 251). Before the advance of Himu towards Delhi and Agra, Bairam, the Regent and *atalik* of the young Akbar (when Humayun died, Akbar was 13 years and 4 months), kept Iskandar Khan Uzbeg at Agra, Tardi Beg Khan at Delhi and Ali Quli Khan Shaibani at Sambal to repel any attack from the end of Himu. Bairam then sent an army to fetch the ladies of Humayun from Kabul to India. But Himu broke off all the three generals of Akbar and occupied Agra and Delhi. It was a very trying moment for both Akbar and Bairam.

Bairam hurriedly called an assembly of nobles who advised the emperor immediately to retreat to Kabut "urging that it was folly to attempt to withstand Himu, now at the head of 100,000 men, with 20,000 which were all that Akbar could muster" (Haig, 1971, 71). But Bairam decided to the contrary and persuaded "the high-spirited and precocious Akbar to adopt this view" (*ibid.*). "One of the reasons as to why did Akbar (or Bairam – SKS) take this vital decision was that his (Akbar's – SKS) future in Afghanistan was equally bleak where his half-brother Mirza Muhammad Hakim was already well-established as the virtual rurler of the country" (Mehta, 141). However, Bamber Gascoigne says that "to bolster the morale of their followers, the prince (Akbar – SKS) and his guardian indulged in some expensive showmanship. The master of ordnance was given instructions to 'prepare fireworks as a treat for the soldiers' and 'to make an image of Hemu, fill it with gunpowder, and set it on fire' " (Gascoigne, 71). Bairam left Khwaja Khizr Khan at Lahore to deal with Sikandar Sur and on 13 October, 1556, advanced with Akbar towards Sirhind where he met with the fugitives from Delhi, including Tardi Beg Khan. The fugitives desired to flee, but Bairam sternly turned down their appeal. Fuss was to be heard in the restive soldiery. To muffle it all over and bring about unity among the covertly refractory nobles, Bairam awarded death penalty to Tardi Beg Khan for fleeing from the fear of Himu, in the absence of the Emperor. Perhaps Bairam's intention of executing Tardi Beg Khan was partly prompted by Bairam's religious considerations. There was a religious difference between Bairam and Tardi Beg, Bairam being an orthodox Shia and Tardi, incidentally Bairam's friend, being a Sunni.

Many historians have condemned this senseless and immoral murder, but Haig says that "Tardi Beg Khan's disgraceful conduct at Delhi merited death according to the military codes of all ages and his advocacy of an immediate retreat from Sirhind rendered his death necessary" (Haig, 1971, 72). Perhaps we should not accept this view of Haig. Firstly, because Tardi Beg's retreat may be construed as a tactical retreat in the face of Himu's pose for a lightning attack on Delhi with a huge army, which in Tardi Beg's calculation it was impossible to repulse. Secondly, the murder was executed without any trial and without giving Tardi Beg a chance for self-defence. Thirdly, Tardi Beg did not flee away like Lakshman Sen at a previous date when Ikhtiar-ud-Din attacked Bengal, but gave battle to Himu, though it was not a full-scale one. Fourthly, Iskandar Khan Uzbek also abandoned Agra as Tardi Beg did Delhi, but Iskandar was absolved of his dereliction of duty. Fifthly, considering Tardi Beg's yeoman's service to Humayun, he might be awarded a less severe punishment. Some historians say that Bairam executed Tardi Beg 'to create an impression on his followers" (Mahajan, 1964, 58). If this be so, then Tardi Beg was used by Bairam only as a means and not as an end, which is quite unethical, and "cruel and totally uncalled for" (Waley, 259). The *Tarikh-i-Daudi* also condemns Bairam's act as "very discreditable" (Dowson, 1955, 84 f.n.).

However, deciding upon a confrontation with Himu, Bairam with Akbar and the Mughal army left Jullundhar (a name coined after the name of Alexander the Great) and reached Thaneswar. Bairam's courage and decision at this time may be compared with that of Babur just before the first battle of Panipat (1526). Had Bairam decided otherwise, the Mughals might have been completely wiped out from India. From Thaneswar the Mughal army moved to the plain of Panipat "where thirty years before Babur had overthrown the Afghan power, and where two centuries later another battle swept away the Maratha power and prepared the way for England" (Kar, 283).

On the side of the Afghans (or, probably, we may say, on the side of the Hindus, because as we have seen in Chapter III, Himu represented the Hindu force), Himu having gained complete victory at Tughlaqabad, occupied Delhi and "sent forward his advance-guard with the greater part of his artillery to Panipat. Akbar's advance division led by Ali Quli Khan came upon this force and by combining deceptive cunning with hard-hitting audacity completely deceived and over-powered the blunt Afghans who fled away abandoning their guns, without making any stand" (Sarkar, Sir, 1970, 67-68). This was the preliminary show-down between the Afghans and the Mughals, before the main battle of Panipat. Stanley Wolpert is of the opinion that "Initially Hemu committed the fatal blunder of sending his entire park of artillery with his weak advance guard to Panipat. Ali Quli Khan Shaibani who led the Mughal advance guard inflicted a severe defeat on Hemu's advance guard, and captured his artillery" (Kar, 284). In spite of this, Himu immediately afterwards launched a severe attack on the Mughal army before it could reach Panipat where the historic battle took place between the Hindu forces (under Himu, the King of Delhi) and the Mughal forces, for the supremacy over Northern India. However, according to De Laet, another battle took place at "Tillepat which is situated between Panipat and Delhi (where – SKS) Ali Quli Khan and Bahadur Khan met Hemu and a Skirmish took place there" (De Laet, 12). After this, the armies of Himu and Akbar met in the field of Panipat.

B

Frederick Augustus beautifully and romantically describes the plain of Panipat thus: "The great military road which runs through Hindustan towards north-western Asia, bisects the broad plain of Panipat at a distance of some 45 to 50 miles ["fifty three miles", according to Kohli (Kohli 13). Mrs. Flora Annie Steel has concurrence (Steel, 173)] north-west from Delhi. Panipat is a far-reaching, almost illimitable level tract, broken only by insignificant undulations. Here and there where shallow soil is moistened by some niggardly water-course, grow sparse grasses and stunted thorn bushes but for the most part the eye falls only on a sterile yellowish-grey waste. Empty silence reigns and it would almost seem that this desert had been created by the battle-field of nations. Here, in the course of ages, the most momentous issues have been fought out; here more than once has the fate of all India been decided; here the Mahabharata places the pre-historic battles of her demigods and heroes; here the knightly Babur won the sovereignty of Hindustan, in a conflict as stubborn as it was decisive; and here now, thirty years later, the fighting power of the Chagatais was arranged to chase the audacious invader to the dominions of his grandson (Akbar – SKS)" (Augustus, 74-75). However, the two armies reached the plain of Panipat on 2nd November, 1556 (Mehta, 141). Himu himself was in the field, and, according to Sir Sarkar, both Akbar and Bairam were "twenty miles behind his (Akbar's – SKS) fighting troops" (Sarkar, Sir, 1970, 68). But, according to Briggs, Akbar "was about two or three *cos* in the rear" (Briggs, 115). About 3,000 picked soldiers guarded Akbar.

Historians differ amongst themselves regarding the strength of Wolpert, "Hemu had three divisions, of which the centre was composed of 20,000 horses (Afghans and Rajputs) supported by 500 elephants and the whole elephantry numbered about 15,000" (Kar, 284). Sir Sarkar gives a detailed and slightly different account: "Undaunted by initial reverse, Himu advanced to the fight, at the head of 30,000 Rajput and Afghan horsemen, comrades of his former victories. His 500 war elehphants were protected by plate armour, and on their backs were placed musketeers and cross-bowmen. The commanders were men of valour and loyalty and pround of their past deeds. But he had no field-gun" (Sarkar, Sir, 1970, 68). On the other hand, "The battle was fought by ten thousand Mughal cavalry under the command of Ali Quli Khan (later created Khan-i-Zaman) and without the help of Babur's profuse fire-arms" (Sarkar, Sir, 1970, 68).

C

The battle-array of both of the sides is described by Sir Sarkar thus : "The Mughal right wing was under Sikandar Khan Uzbak, the left under Abdullah Khan Uzbak, the centre under Ali Quli Khan Shaibani, and the vanguard under Husain Quli Beg and Shah Quli

The Second Battle of Panipat

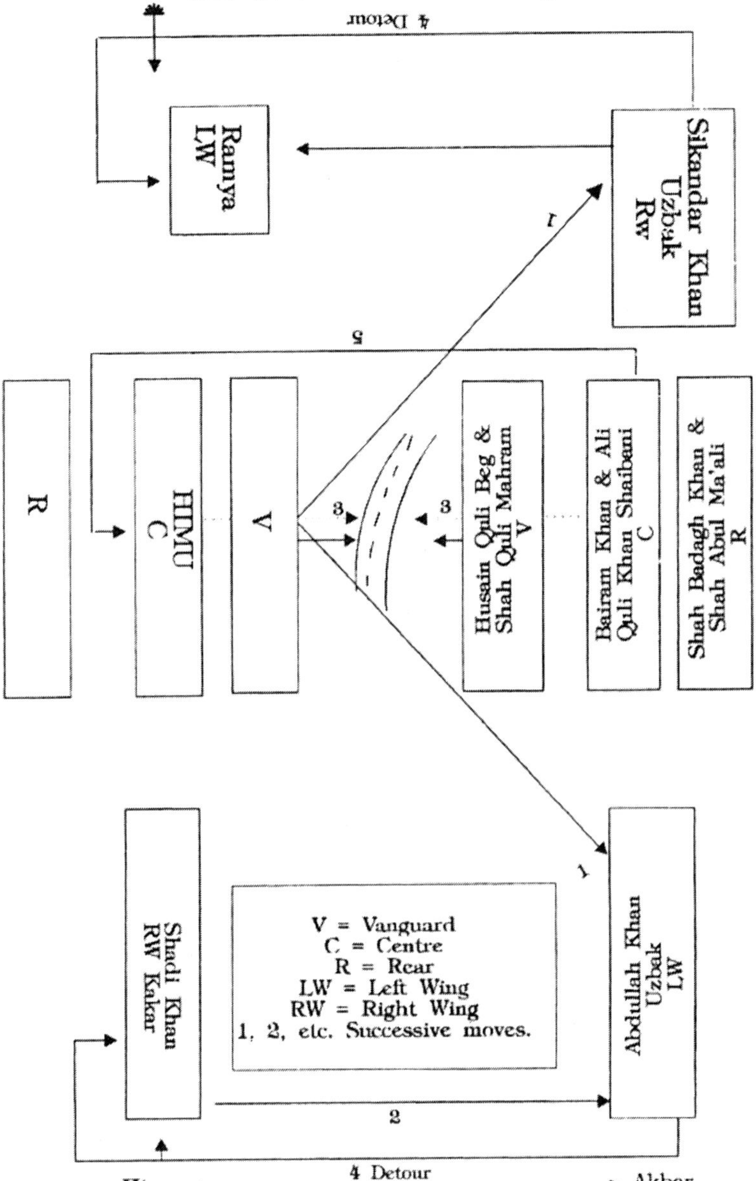

This sketch was not done by anybody, before.

Mahram (with Bairam's own contingent of Turks). Himu took post in the centre and gave the charge of his right wing to Shadi Khan Kakar and his left to Ramya (his own sister's son)" (Sarkar, Sir, 1970, 68). In the advance guard of the Mughals, there were such other valiant commanders as Ally Kooly Khan Indijany, Mahomed Khan Budukshy, Mujnoon Khan Kakshal. The advance guard was supported by Hoossein Kooly Beg, Mohamed Sadik Khan Purwanchy, Shah Kooly Khan Mahrum, Meer Mahomed Barka, Kasim Khan Nyshapoory, Syed Mahomed Barka and others. The army of Himu took the western side of the field and the Mughal army the eastern side.

The battle-formations of both the armies are being shown in the accompanying sketch. (Such a sketch has not so far been drawn by any historian. Even Lt. Col. Kar, who has shown in sketches the formations of many battles in his book *The Military History of India,* has not drawn the sketch of the battle-formations of the second battle of Panipat.)

D

Sir H.M. Elliot has narrated two very enchanting stories about Himu before his going to the battle-field of Panipat. The first is this: "When he (Himu – SKS) was going to fight on the field of Panipat, the night before the battle, he beheld, in a dream, a torrent came down and carry away the elephant on which he was mounted. When he was nearly drowned, a Mughal came, cast a chain round his neck, and drew him out. On awaking, he sent for the interpreters of dream, related his to them, and asked them to explain it. The interpreters, after thinking over the business, looked at one another, and Himun (Himu – SKS) inferred that there was something unpleasant in the explanation. He therefore said, 'Banish fear from your minds, tell what you have discovered.' The interpreters said, 'The torrent which you saw in the Mughal army *(sic)*, which comes with such force that it carries away you and the horse on which you are mounted (could Himu ride on a horse?– SKS) and the chain signifies the blood which will flow from your body when you are wounded, and cover you entirely.' Himun became fearful and said, 'The very reverse of this dream will happen'." (*infra*). This reminds one of the dream of Julius Caesar before his death.

The second story runs thus: "On the morrow, when he (Himu – SKS) mounted to proceed to battle, heavy rain fell, and the best elephant of that *infidel*, which was of gigantic size, was struck in two by lightning. On account of this, Himun became very thoughtful, and aware that the good fortune of the Mughals was in the ascendant, and that victory was not for him, he was much terrified at the explanation of his dream, and set forth unwillingly to the fight." (Dowson, 88) (emphasis added). Lest some one may question the authenticity of the stories, Elliot adds : "We have seen elsewhere that a similar event is said to have preceded the battle of Ambala between the Niazis and the imperialists" (Dowson, 88). But, we think, these stories were either narrated to Elliot or the historian himself invented these on the model of the dream of Shakespeare's Julius Caesar. The stories are not above question. Firstly, because, Elliot writes that during the battle of Panipat "Himun was excessively arrogant" (Dowson, 90). How then could he be "very thoughtful" and "much terrified" in the battle? *(supra)*. Secondly, sometimes, Elliot is not a very dependable historian. Take for example, on p. 86 of his *The History of India as Told By Its Own Historians*, he says that the Mughal cavalry was 26,000 strong, but on p. 88, as justly pointed out by John Dowson, he says that it did not exceed 20,000. Perhaps Elliot did not care much for apodicticity. Lastly, his religious arthodoxy [he calls Himu an infidel *(supra)*] may have helped him in the invention of stories about Himu.

However, before the battle Bairam Khan "made an inspiring speech (as Babur did before the first battle of Panipat – SKS) to his officers, pointing out that they must conquer or perish, and his brave words were supported by the divination of a soothsayer who deduced favourable omens from his inspection of the shoulder-blade of a sheep." (Smith, 28).

We may imagine that the battle began with cries like "*Allahu Akbar*" (God is great) and "Din! Din!" (The Faith! The Faith!) on the part of the Muslims [Akbar later on used the war cry Ya Mu'in! (O, Helper!)] and "Gopal! Gopal!" (Maratha cry) or "Har, Har, Mahadeo" on the part of the Hindus (Irvine, 232). Perhaps the Muslim soldiers on both the sides used Muslim war cries as the Hindu soldiers used Hindu war cries on both the sides, and so there was no common war cry of the Mughals and of the soldiers of Himu. Whatever might be the war cries, the battle of those days was a confusion of action and noise, as Isaiah says, " 'every battle of the warrior is with confused noise'." (Irvine, 231).

Some of the weapons used by both the sides were *tir, kaman,* (another type of bow), *phalakhan* (sling), *tup* (gun), *tapanchah* (pistol), *bara tup* (big gun), *gupta* (catapault), *nizah* (spear or lance), *sabra* (axe), *dhal* (shield), *gardany* (a kind of sword), *ban* (rocket), *chaku* (knife), *chaku* (another kind of knife), tabar (*war axe*), etc.

According to Sir Sarkar, the Armageddon of the Second Battle of Panipat was a "ding-dong fight" (*infra*). The decisive battle was fought at a place "about four miles north-west of the scene of Babur's victory" (*infra*). On 5th November, 1556, "The battle began with an attack by Himu. The onset of the furious elephants shook the right and left wings of the Mughal army and many hard-fighting warriors fell on their side. The survivors did not flee, but Turk-like withdrew from the frontal fighting to avoid the elephants, and making a detour fell on the enemy horsemen's flanks, galling them with their superior archery and shaking them by their Parthian wheeling tactics. The Mughal centre too advanced, but coming to a plot of ground with a deep ravine in front, which was impassable for elephants, it stood on the defensive plying its missile weapons on the foe powerless to reach it with either horse or elephant. "Meanwhile the flanking parties of Turks, mounted on superb horses, had penetrated the enemy ranks from side and rear and were slashing at the elephants' legs or shooting off their drivers. As the Afghan attack slackened and the elephants fell back, Ali Quli led his cavalry out of its shelter and making a detour attacked the Afghan centre from behind. Himu who was surveying the battle field and directing the operations from the back of a lofty elephant, hastened to the threatened side, making every effort to restore the battle and 'leaving no strategem or heroic deed that his mind could conceive unattempted' (*Akbarnamah*, ii, 64). He made repeated counter-charges with his powerful elephants, overthrowing the Mughals in the direct line of his advance. But the war was taking toll of his strength; two of his bravest lieutenants, Bhagwan Das and Shadi Khan Kakar were killed before his eyes. The mixed fighting raged most stubbornly for some time, when an arrow pierced his eye" (Sarkar, Sir, 1970, 68-69) as Harold was shot in the eye by an arrow in the battle of Hastings (1066 A.D.), 490 years ago (Carter and Mears, 80). We may remember here that Anandapal in his battle with Subuktagin was also harassed by arrows shot from the side of the Muslims. Anandapal's elephant "under arrows and naptha-balls became unruly and turned and fled" (Vaidya, 47). As a result Anandapal was vanquished.

Before this, writes Rawlinson, Himu "was successful in routing the flanks of his enemy's army, and might even have won [The war – SKS]" (Rawlinson, 174). According to Kasim Ferista, initially, Himu was not very successful : "Hemoo began the action with his elephants, in hopes of alarming the enemy's cavalry, unaccustomed to these animals; but the Moguls attacked them so furiously, after they had penetrated even to the centre of the army, where Khan Zuman Khan commanded, that, galled with lances, arrows, and javelins, they became quite unruly, and disdaining the control of their drivers, turned and threw the Afghan ranks into confusion. Hemoo mounted on an elephant of prodigious size, still continued the action with great bravery, at the head of four thousand horse, in the very midst of the Mogul army; but being pierced through the eye with an arrow, he sunk into his howda from extreme agony" (Ferista, 114-115). Adolf Waley writes that the battle was started off by Himu: "As he gave the signal to advance, the elephants, 500 in number, trumpeting loudly, charged full into the centre of the Mughal army, which at that very point was commanded by Bairam Khan in person. The terrific impact caused the troops to stagger, but their Commander proved equal to the occasion and ordered the Mughal archers to concentrate and to aim at the faces of the officers who were mounted on the elephants" (Waley, 260). G.B. Malleson differs from Waley a little bit and says that Himu first attacked the Mughal left. His description of the proceeding of the battle runs thus : "Hemu had divided his army into three divisions. In front marched the five hundred elephants, each bestridden by an officer of rank, and led by Hemu, on his own favourite animal, in person. He dashed first against the advancing left wing of the Mughals and threw it into disorder, but as his lieutenants failed to support the attack with infantry, he drew off, and threw himself on the centre, commanded by Bairam in person. That astute general had directed his archers in anticipation of such an attack, to direct their arrows at the faces of the riders. One of these arrows pierced the eye of Hemu, ..." (Hunter, 69-70). According to *The New Encyclopaedia Britannica*, "Hemu, at the head of 30,000 men, overthrew the Mughal right and left wings and launched an attack on the enemy centre, hurling 1,500 elephants against it. The Mughals were about to give way when Hemu was struck in the eye by an arrow and fell unconscious on his elephant" (*The New Ency. Brit.*, vol. 9, p. 379). It is curious to note that in 712 King Dahir was defeated by Mahmud because Dahir's elephant was shot by an arrow with burning cotton on its head. The elephant took to flight causing pell-mell in the soldiery of Dahir. Afterwards Dahir himself was struck by an arrow and fell down" (Haig, 1965, vol. 3, 5).

We can gather some additional information regarding the actions and movements of the battle from Lt. Col. Kar. He writes "The right and left wing of the Mughal army were overthrown by an attack of Hemu's elephants, and defeat stared them (The Mughals – SKS) in the face. Hemu led the advance on his elephants. Fortunately the Mughal centre under Ali Quli Khan Shaibani remained firm, and a small contingent under a few brave Commanders like Muhammad Qasim Khan Nishapuri and Lal Khan Badakshi made a wide detour and launched an attack on Hemu's rear [Sir Sarkar differs from Kar. According to him, the Mughal army attacked Himu's centre and not rear (Sarkar, Sir, 1970, 69)]. The [Mughal–SKS] centre as a whole moved forward and reached a spot which had so wide a ravine in front that it could not be crossed by Hemu's elephants. Thus the Mughals got the opportunity of making an effective use of its arrows and bullets against the elephants which were held back because of the ravine. Taking advantage of this the flanking parties of Turks, mounted on horses, made a wide detour and took the enemy ranks from side and rear and were slashing at the elephants' legs or shooting off their drivers. Seeing this Hemu advanced to the threatened front and tried to retrieve the situation. The battle raged fiercely and two of Hemu's generals, Bhagwan Das and Shadi Khan fell in the field. He launched vigorous charges with his elephants and was about to carry the day" (Kar, 284).

V.A. Smith is of the opinion that Himu was deprived by an "accident" of his " 'victory, throne and life' " (*infra*) ; but Sir Wolseley Haig is certain about it (Majumdar, 1984, 101). Himu was not Maginot-minded; he made pre-emptive strikes on the Mughals. His moves during the opening stage of the war was logistically appreciable. He whisked his vanguard and smashed the frontal feature of the Mughals. But he aught not had charged the confusing defiles of arrow-shooting Mughals leaving the rest of his army to its fate. However, De Laet's charge against Himu that he "had not paid his soldiers" (*infra*) and so they "were grumbling and unwilling to fight; and did not obey orders" (De Laet, 12) is unfounded as this is not supported by any other historian.

E

As ill luck would have it, Himu was struck in the eye by an arrow, taken prisoner-of-war wound and unconscious like Rana Sanga 29 years ago in the battle of Khanwa (Mehta, 103), brought before Akbar, and executed. All these are delineated by several historians, differently. Let us follow some of the important historians. This may also give us an insight, by the by, into how far historians may differ among themselves, and withal establish the fact that history has to be continuously re-written.

(i) Lt. Col. H.C. Kar writes that Himu "was hit in the eye by an arrow and rendered unconscious" (Kar, 284).

(ii) Sir Jadhunath Sarkar says that "the mixed fighting raged most stubbornly for some time, when an arrow pierced his (Himu's – SKS) eye. The blood spouting from the wound was seen by Afghans near him, but he pulled the arrow out, bandaged the eye with a scarf, and ordered the fight to go on, after which he fell down into the *howda* in a faint" (Sarkar, Sir, 1970, 69).

(iii) S.C. Sarkar and K.K. Datta almost concurs with Sir Sarkar. They say that "a stray arrow decided the day. Himu was struck by it in the eye, and became unconscious in his *howdah*" (Sarkar and Datta, as 1942, 56).

(iv) J.L. Mehta writes that "an accidental shot hit Hem Chandra in the eye and made him unconscious. It created panic among his soldiers who, taking him to be dead, fled the field. The *mahavat* of Hem Chandra's elephant tried his best to save his master by withdrawing from the battle front, but Shah Kuli Mehram, a Mughal soldier, gave him a hot chase and overpowered him. Hem Chandra's body was covered with blood when he was presented before Akbar in a state of unconsciousness" (Mehta, 143).

(v) According to R.C. Majumdar : "Probably he [Himu–SKS] would have won [The battle – SKS] but for the accident that he was struck in the eye by an arrow which pierced his brain and rendered him unconscious" (Majumdar, 1984, 100).

(vi) Sir Wolseley Haig says that Himu's eye had "been pierced by an arrow so well directed that its point projected from the back of his head. His troops at once dispersed. "Shah Quli Khan Mahram, a Baharlu Turk in Bairam Khan's service, who afterwards attained to the commands of 3500 horse, came up with Himu's elephant, Hawai, as the driver endeavouring to carry his master beyond the reach of danger. He begged Shah Quli not to slay him and told him who the elephant's wounded rider was. Shah Quli at once caused Himu to be led to Akbar, who had by now appeared on the field" (Haig, 1971, 72).

(vii) Vincent Smith is of the opinion that Himu was "struck in the eye by an arrow which pierced his brain and rendered him unconscious .... Hemu's elephant, which had fled into the jungle, was brought back by Shah Quli Khan Mahram, and its unconscious rider was placed before the Protector [Bairam – SKS] and Akbar, who had ridden up" (Smith, 29).

(viii) Kasim Ferista gives a different description. He says that Himu "being pierced through the eye with an arrow, he sunk into his howda from extreme agony. The greater part of his troops feared his wound was mortal, and forsook him. Raising himself again, Hemoo drew the arrow and with it the eye out of the socket, which he wrate [*sic*] in his handkerchief, and in spite of his painful situation, he continued to fight with unabated courage, endeavouring with the few men who remained about his person, to force his retreat through the enemy's line. At length Shah Kolly Khan Mahram levelled his lance against the driver of Hemoo's elephant, who, in order to save his own life, pointed to his master, and promised Shah Kolly Khan to guide the elephant wherever he directed" (Briggs, 115).

(ix) Ferista's account is supported by Frederick Augustus (Augustus, 76).

(x) But H.M. Elliot writes : ".... it chanced that, by the decree of the Almighty, an arrow struck Himun [Himu – SKS] in the *forehead*. He told his elephant driver to take the elephant out of the field of battle ...... When Shah Kuli Beg was told of what had occurred, he came up to the elephant, and brought it into the presence of Bairam Khan. Bairam Khan, after prostating himself, and returning thanks, caused Himun to descend from the elephant, after which he bound his hands, and took him before the young and fortunate Prince, ..." (*italics* mine) (Dowson, 1955, 90).

(xi) Some Soviet historians, for example Koko Antonov, Gregori Bongard-Levin and Gregori Kotovsky, add that Himu fell from the back of the elephant after being shot in the eye with an arrow (Antonov, 315).

(xii) G.B. Malleson is of the opinion that Himu's elephant's "driver had been killed" (Hunter, 70).

So we find that almost all the historians agree that Himu was struck in the eye by a stray arrow. But Elliot says that he was shot in the forehead and not in the eye. All agree that it was Shah Quli Khan Mahram who brought Himu to Akbar. Some say that Himu pulled out the arrow ; some deny it. However, we can probably make out the fact thus. Himu was struck in the eye and fell on the *howda* of his huge elephant called Hawai, and on seeing this (as it happened in all the battles of bygone days that as soon as the commander was killed, soldiers disappeared confusedly), the soldiers of Himu spade away post haste and pell-mell. Shah Quli Khan Mahram-i-Baharlu, a distant relative of Bairam and Commander of the Mughal vanguard, surmising that it might be Himu who was shot at fell on the *howda*, made wide detour round the ravine (this was missed by historians) and arrived at the spot. Shah Quli at first could not identify the wounded man and so asked the driver of the elephant (*mahut*) to spell out who it was, on pain of death. The bewildered driver who had been endeavouring to take his master to a safe place, told Shah Quli that it was Himu the same. Shah Quli immediately forced the driver to take the elephant with Himu on its back, panting unconsciously, to where Akbar and Bairam were waiting under a luxurious canopy, to take stock of the profit and loss of the great battle. Elliot's description of the elaborate courtesy shown by Shah Quli Khan to the unconscious Himu is probably not true. It is debated whether Himu's driver himself drove the beast to Akbar or the driver was killed by the Mughals and one of them drove it. Adolf Waley says,

"The driver of Hemu's elephant had been killed and the powerful beast, with the unconscious general still in the howdah, was captured by a small body of Mughal cavalry" (Waley, 260). William Erskine and J.L. Mehta support this view.

F

Soon after Himu was brought to the presence of Akbar, the P.O.W. was executed. Historians hold two different opinions regarding the way Himu was executed.

(i) According to Kasim Ferista, who was a contemporary of Akbar, "When Hemoo was brought in the presence (of Akbar – SKS), Beiram Khan recommended the King to do a meritorious act by killing the infidel with his own hand. Akbar, in order to fulfil the wish of his minister, drew his sword, and touched the *head* of the captive and became entitled to the appellation of Ghazy, while Beiram Khan, drawing his own sabre, at a single blow severed the head of Hemoo from his body" (italics mine) (Briggs, 115). V.A. Smith gives a similar description : " 'Bairam Khan desired Akbar to earn the title of Ghazi, or slayer of the infidel, by flashing his sword on the captive. The boy naturally obeyed his guardian and smote Himu on the neck with his scimitar. The bystanders also plunged their swords into the bleeding corpse" (Smith, 29). This reminds one of the murder of Julius Caesar. According to V.A. Smith, Akbar's "unwillingness to strike a helpless prisoner" was "the late invention of courtly flatterers" (*ibid*). Sir Haig, quoting J.R. A.S. of 1916 (p. 527), says that "the boy [Akbar – SKS] severed Himu's head from his body" (Haig, 1971, 72), but he adds that "according to another version [Akbar – SKS] merely touched the infidel, who was slain by those in attendance" (*ibid.*). H.M. Elliot agrees with V.A. Smith and says that to persuade Akbar to kill Himu, Bairam said " 'As this is your first success, let your Highness's own august hand smite this infidel with the sword.' The Prince, accordingly, struck him [Himu – SKS], and divided his head from his unclean body (Nov. 5, A.D. 1556)" (Dowson, 90). Lt. Col. Kar also says that Akbar himself "severed Hemu's head from the body" and opines that "the story that he refused to comply with Bairam's instructions seems to be the late invention of courtly flatterers" (Kar, 284).

(ii) On the other hand, some historians do not admit that Akbar himself killed Himu or even touched Himu's neck with a scimitar.

Fredrick Augustus says that Bairam Khan "asked the Emperor to strike off the prisoner's [Himu's – SKS] head and thus by slaying an infidel, win for himself the elevated title of Ghazi; but the generous boy could not bring himself to kill a fallen and captive foe. To end the delay and to accustom his sovereign to the sight of blood, Bairam himself shore off Hemu's head" (Augustus, 76). P. Kohli and K. Nanda agree with Augustus. They write thus : "Merciful by nature, the young kind [*sic* = King – SKS] refused [to kill Himu – SKS] saying 'he is now no better than a dead-man; how can I strike him ? If he had strength I would try my sword and cut off his head" (Kohli, 14). Flora Annie Steel also believes that the mecriful Akbar did not slay Himu himself at the instance of Bairam. In her native facile and tell-story style, she gives a beautiful and picturesque description of the event. She writes that Bairam Khan, "The savage old Tartar general brought him [Himu – SKS] into Akbar's tent, and, presenting the boy with a sword, said : 'This is your first war, my King. Prove your sword upon this infidel.' But Akbar drew back indignatly. 'How can I strike one who is no better than a dead man?' He replied hotly. 'It is on strength and sense that a King's sword is tried.' Whereupon Bairam, incensed, no doubt, by the proud refusal, instantly cut down Hemu himself. "They say the boy-King wept; certain it is that he never forgot, never quite forgave, the incident" (Steel, 173). Adolf Waley concurs with Steel and says that "Even these noble words [of Akbar – SKS] failed to stir any feeling of pity for a fallen enemy in Bairam Khan's fierce heart, and in the presence of the Emperor, who shrank from him in horror, he drew his sword and slew the striken captive with his own hand. This outrage widened the rift between Akbar and his adviser, which had first been caused by the execution of Tardi Beg" (Waley, 260).

It is really very difficult to say certainly which of the two sorts of opinions is correct. Therefore R.C. Majumdar leaves it an open question (Majumdar, 1967, 439). But Vincent Smith, probably, is not right in taking the boy Akbar for an ordinary kid. Smith says, "nor is there any good reason for supposing that at that time the boy [Akbar – SKS) was more scrupulous than his officers. The official story, ... seems to be the late invention of courtly flatterers ....." (Smith, 29). We know from the noted historian, Makhan Lal Roychaudhury (vide his *Akbar*, *passim*) that Akbar, even in his teens, showed some signs uncommon in boys of his age. At 21 he was deeply meditative. His refractoriness was observed even in his early years. To smite the captive and unconscious Himu was not a matter of strategic expediency (as Smith conceived) but it was a matter of the heart. Further, it was not long after the execution of Himu that there developed a wide difference between Akbar and Bairam. Akbar might have had a soft corner in his heart for the Hindus as he might have remembered the protection of a Hindu in which he was born. The presence of the helpess Himu might have ignited his memory at the particular moment. So Akbar's refusal to obey Bairam may not be unfounded. Even "*The Tarikh-i-Daudi and many other historians say the young Prince declined to commit this wanton act of brutality, and his subsequent actions render this highly probable*" (italics mine) (Dowson, 90).

G

After the execution, "Himu's head was sent to Kabul to be exposed (for what purpose, we do not know – SKS) and his body was gibbeted at Delhi as a warning to those who would resist Bairam Khan and Akbar" (Sarkar and Datta, 56). "In accordance with the ghastly custom of the times, a tower was built with the heads of the slain" (Smith, 29). This ghastly custom was probably imported into India by the Turks. We may remember here that in the first battle of Panipat the head of the dead Sultan Ibrahim Lodi was severed and presented to Babur (Tripathi, 34). Years after the 2nd battle of Panipat, on 12 August, 1576, Daud's head was also severed from his body and presented to Akbar as a trophy (Mehta, 184). However, the revenge of the Mughals did not end there. The Mughal forces conquered Alwar where Himu's family lived. Akbar earned the title of *ghazi* and entered Delhi and immediately detached Peer Mahomed Khan, the steward of Bairam Khan's household, towards Mewat wherein the treasure of Himu was deposited. Himu's father "was captured [by Mulla Pir Muhammad – SKS] and brought alive before Nasir-al-mulk. The latter called upon him to change his religion. The old man answered, 'for eighty years I have worshipped my God, according to this religion. Why should I, merely from fear of my life, and without understanding it come into your way of worship ?' Pir Muhammad treated his words as if he heard them not, and answered him with the tongue of the sword" (Majumdar, 1984, 101). This reminds one of another such case of a Brahman during the time of Sikandar Lodi. The Brahman preached that Hindusim and Islam both were true. The courtiers "decided that since the Brahman had admitted the truth of

Islam he should be invited to embrace it, with the alternative of death in the event of refusal. The decision commanded itself to Sikandar and the penalty was exacted from the Brahman, who refused to change his faith" (Haig, 240). Earlier we have seen that Himu's father, Puran Das, left hearth and home for other-worldly pursuits. We do not know how he came back to Himu and lived with or near him.

The Mughals could not capture Himu's wife. She "had ascaped from Delhi into Mewat, taking with her all his [Himu's – SKS] treasure" (Haig, 73). Pir Muhammad was sent in pursuit of her but in vain. We do not know what occurred to Ramya, Himu's nephew, who had been fighting beside Himu. Perhaps he was slain in the battle-field.

After the battle 1,500 elephants of Himu were captured by the Mughals. They also slew many fugitives and took much plunder. Smith writes : "The pursuit of the defeated army being vigorously pressed, the victors next day without halting, marched straight to Delhi, which opened its gates to Akbar, who made his entry in state. Agra also passed into his possession. In accordance with the ghastly custom of the times, a tower was built with the heads of the slain" (Smith, 29). For about a month, the Emperor remained at Delhi.

From Delhi Akbar "sent thence a force into Mewat to pursue the broken army of Hemu and to gain the large amount of treasure it was conveying" (Malleson, in Hunter, 84). After that Akbar turned his gaze towards his rival Sikandar Sur. From Sirhind, Akbar and Bairam Khan proceeded towards Lahore and laid seige on it. Sikandar withstood a long seige but ultimately surrendered at Mankot in Jammu (modern Ramkot) in May, 1557. Sikandar was well treated and offered "Kharid and Bihar districts as a fief" (Smith, 30). After about two years Sikandar died reducing the Afghan-Mughal tension to its nadir.

H

The long-drawn rivalry between the Afghans and the Mughals for the supremacy over Northern India soon vanished, though not absolutely. The coping stone of the Mughal Empire in the true sense of the term was sown by Akbar "for no Mughal empire had previously existed in spite of attempts to create one" (Davies, Collin, 1975, 44). The Afghan hope was almost completely shattered and with that the

Hindu hope of revival. Battles between the Afghans and the Mughals were no more heard of till the 17th and the 18th centuries, though conflicts in the shape of skirmishes between the Afghans and the Mughals continued for some time (Khan, 29). The Afghans began to develop rapport with the services in the Mughal army. But the general tension did not completely subside as we see that even "Mughal padishah Aurangzeb had to fight against the Afghan tribes for almost two years" (Progress Publishers, 107). Muhammad Adil Shah was killed in 1557 in an encounter with the ruler of Bengal. Adil, therefore ruled for about four years – from the death of Firuz in 1553 to 1557. On the other hand Ibrahim Khan had withdrawn and sought "an asylum in Orissa" (*The Encyclopaedia Britannica*, vol. 9, p. 379). "The stormy career of the Sur dynasty thus came to an end, and Akbar was left free to consolidate his dominion undisturbed by the claims of rivals to his sovereignty, except in so far as his younger brother, Muhammad Hakim of Kabul, made feeble attempts from time to time to contest the throne of Hindustan" (Smith, 30). "The victory of Panipat, though it did not bring with it the subjugation of all of Akbar's foes, and though he had many perils yet to face, established him, permanently upon the throne of Hindustan" (Waley, 260). After his capture of Delhi and Agra, as we have seen, Akbar launched a military expedition against Sikandar Shah Sur who after ensconsing himself for some time in the fastness of Mankot in the Sewaliks, was compelled "to make his personal submission to the Emperor. (Waley, 261). It may be added here that historians differ on the question about the evening of Adil Shah's life. Historians generally admit that he died in 1557 in Bengal in an encounter with Pir Muhammad Khan of Sherwan. But, according to Michael Edwards, he died at Monghyr in 1556 (Edwardes, 324).

I

In spite of the army of Himu being less trained in warfare and less disciplined, Himu was about to carry out the day, when ill luck fell upon him in the shape of a stray arrow piercing his eye. Nevertheless, Himu cannot be absolved of a great logistic blunder immediately before the main encounter with the Mughals in the field of Panipat. Himu had sent his park of artillery to Panipat without the normal complement of supporting force and without any lodgement. Ali Quli Khan-i-Shaibani, formerly a subordinate officer to Tardi Beg, rode off from another direction with a cavalry ten thousand strong with the speed of a flying arrow and captured the whole park of artillery "which had been obtained at great cost from Turkey" (Waley, 259), almost without any resistance by the army of Himu. J.L. Mehta heaps the responsibilities for the defeat of Himu on Himu himself and withal questions Himu's efficiency as a general: "The most important single factor which led to his fall was his ignorance of the war strategy and his shortsightedness as military general. As a matter of fact, immediately after his occupation of Agra and Delhi, he could have chased the handful of Mughals out of India without much difficulty ; it was because the Mughals, at that time, were regarded as foreign intruders while Hem Chandra enjoyed confidence and support of various sections of the Indian society – Hindus and Muslims alike" (Mehta, 143-44). It seems, Mehta is quite correct here. Himu had the capability of wiping out the remaining Mughal forces after the battle of Tughlaqabad, but he indulged in paranoid grandeur after occupying the throne of Delhi. Again, he committed a great blunder by sending the park of artillery unsupported. The Mughals easily captured it and thus put the Afghan forces there out of commission and consequently the Mughals could occupy some dominant features of the field of Panipat. Further, Himu was too peremptory in rushing to the dangerous front during the action; the supreme commander has to supervise the action of the army as a whole, and should not have been overtly engaged in any particular front of the theatre. But, in spite of all these, how can we say that Himu wanted military genius, knowing full well that he is said to have fought as many as twenty-two battles and won them all?

CHAPTER V

The Hindus *Vis-a-vis* The Afghans and The Mughals During The Time of Himu

Historians, so far, have interpreted the period roughly between 1526 to 1556 chiefly as the period of conflicts between the Afghans and the Mughals, for the overlordship of Northern India. But, besides the Afghans and the Mughals, there was another force – the Hindus, and the period witnessed four types of conflicts : (i) Afghan-Mughal conflicts, (ii) Hindu-Mughal conflicts, (iii) Afghan-Hindu conflicts, and (iv) conflicts between the Mughals on the one hand and the combined Hindu and Afghan forces on the other. The strivings of the Hindus for freedom and self-determination as well as for the revival of their lost supremacy, have received scant justice from historians, so far. It is not true that the Hindus absolutely compromised with the Muslim domination in India after 712, lying supine. This will be clear and evident if we study the history of the period a wee bit closely.

The immigration of Muslims into India was not a new phenomenon in the 8th century. Muslims of Arabia had contacted India long ago. "The earliest Muslims came to India as traders and mystics during the very first century of the Hijri era. They arrived on the Western coast from lands across the Arabian Sea; some bringing with them merchandise for exchange with local produce; others carrying the message of the Prophet of Islam" (Ministry of Information and Broadcasting, Govt. of India, 1982). Another cause of Muslim immigration into India was the fear for the Mughals. "This [The Delhi Sultanate – SKS] was followed by a remarkable influx into India of Muslim intellectuals, mystics, saints, scholars and men of affairs who were either seeking refuge from the scourge of the Mongol invasion of their homelands or were attracted to immigrate to India by the new opportunity for employment and advancement" (*ibid.*). The Hindus did not stand on their way; they only did so when the Muslims wanted to rule over Hindustan and become their overlords.

However, the four-fold type of conflicts among the Hindus, the Afghans and the Mughals may be graphically represented thus:

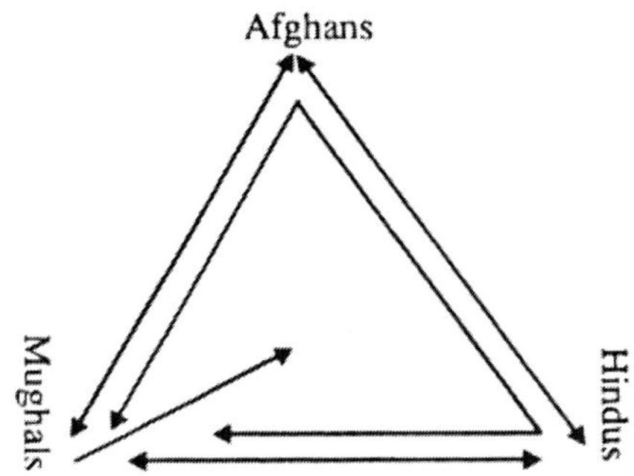

The Afghans and the Mughals stood sharply against each other, though sometimes the Mughals recruited Afghan soldiers. The comparatively weaker Hindu power intended profit out of Afghan-Mughal conflicts. Due to their long habitation in India the Afghans merged themselves into the general social and cultural mainstream of the country. As a result, there were fewer conflicts between the Hindus and the Afghans, than those between the Afghans and the Mughals or between the Hindus and the Mughals. Further, we do not find any instance where the Hindus fought the Afghans jointly with the Mughals, or where the Mughals foufght against the Hindus jointly with the Afghans.

I

(The Afghan-Mughal Conflicts)

We have seen the Afghan-Mughal conflicts in Chapter II. Here we shall only record some comments on these conflicts.

When the Afghans first began to come down from the high rocky Afghanistan to the plains of India, we do not know. India being a bordering land of plenty and Afghanistan being a land of several dearths, the Afghans gradually and imperceptibly entered into India, and in course of time merged themselves in the main cultural stream of the country. They were, so to say, naturalised and accepted by the Indian brethren as fellow citizens. All told, the Afghans ruled Northern India for about 92 years. The First Afghan House or the Lodi Empire ruled from 1451 (when Bahlul Lodi seized power from Ala-ud-din, the last Sayyid King) to 1526; and the Second Afghan House or the Sur Empire ruled from 1539 (battle of Chausa) or from 1540 (battle of Kanauj) to 1556 (the Second Battle of Panipat). The naturalised Afghans were not "savages" as Winston Churchill in his *My Early Life* (p. 26) says. But the story is otherwise with the Mughals. They gate-crashed into India showing every sort of violence, and as such were mightily opposed by the united forces of the Afghans and the Hindus. Even after their victory in the first battle of Panipat, the Mughals were not accepted as the lords of Northern India. Sarkar and Datta rightly divide the Muslims into native Muhammedans and foreign Muhammedans. According to them, the Afghans were the native ones. They wrote : "The victory of Panipat had made Babar the master of Delhi, but the Afghan nobles were seething in discontent against the new Mughal rule ..... It was Sher Shah who worked out this Afghan or rather Indo-Moslem national revival, and effected a temporary but glorious restoration of native Muhammedan rule in India" (Sarkar and Datta, 34). Yet, ironically, Babur "came down to the great plains [of India – SKS] at the invitation of the Afghan rajas" (Weech, 329). According to *The Tezkereh al Wakiat* of Jouhar, it was Humayun and not Babur, who engaged the Afghans for the first time: "When Babur invaded Hindustan (A.H. 932, A.D. 1525), he gave the command of the right wing of his army to Humayun, and he was the first general that engaged the Afghans" (Stewart, v).

In fact, the Afghans had anti-Mughal attitude even before the beginning of the second Afghan Empire. The cause was the exploitation of the Afghan *Khamsayas* (dependents) by the Mughals (Progress Publishers, 103). The Afghan anti-Mughal attitude was hardened during the time of Babur, because he dealt with them "cruelly" (*op. cit.*, 99). The Afghans as well as the Hindus treated the Mughals as foreigners. The Afghan attitude towards the Mughals is evident in the dying declaration of Sher Shah (*supra*, Chapter I). Before the Surs, the Lodis also wanted to stave the Mughals off India. The slave Kings, the Khaljis and the Lodis also kept constant watch on Mughal invasion of India. All this has been discussed above. We can only remember here Ala-ud-din Khalji's hatred for the Mughals. When the New Muslims, who were newly proselytised Turks settled around Delhi, rebelled against Ala-ud-din, the King caused about 30 thousand of them killed in the space of only one day. Another case of Ala-ud-din's hatred for the Mughals may be cited here. The Mongol or Mughal ruler Uljaitu Sultan was once anxious to establish diplomatic relations with Ala-ud-din. "But the Mongol ruler's proposal of marrying a Delhi princess evidently so annoyed Alauddin that he had the ambassador imprisoned and some of their attendents trodden under the feet of elephants" (*Journal of Indian History*, Univ. of Kerala, Trivandrum, vol. LI, Pt. III, Dec. 1973, pp. 591-92).

In 1526, it was the Lodi branch of the Afghans, who were defeated by Babur. Curiously enough, when Babur wanted to invade India, both the Hindus and the Afghans extended their supports to him. Rana Sanga promised to help Babur against Ibrahim Lodi, of course for his own gains. In the same way, Alam Khan Lodi, uncle of Ibrahim Lodi, also promised to extend his help to Babur. But, in the end, before the battle, both withdrew their words. Sher Shah's heart went with the Lodis for the latter's anti-Mughal attitude, as is evident in his fourth dying declaration: "The last is, to have raised a tomb to Ibrahim Lodi in Panipat ......" (Elliot, 143). We may remember here that Bahadur Shah of Gujrat also had a plan "to cripple the Mughal empire by attacking it at different points" (Tripathi, 75). The extent of the hatred that the Afghans bore for the Mughals can be inferred from the fact that Ibrahim Lodi's mother poisoned Babur not only because he killed her son but also because Babur was Mughal. Babur survived providentially. But if he did not, the Mughal hope would go for ever. Mehta writes : "The stars were favourable to Babur for had he been murdered nothing could have saved the Kingdom, which he was building up, and *the Rajputs would have been supreme in Hindustan*." (emphasis added) (Mehta, 39).

After 1526, the Afghans and the Mughals were in constant conflicts, as we have seen in Chapter II. It may be noted here that there were both Afghan and Hindu soldiers in the service of the Mughals. It is possible that there were also Mughal soldiers, though very few, in the pay-rolls of the Afghans and the Hindus. This was so because in those days, the feeling of nationality was not very strong. People would take services considering only better service conditions. Yet, on the whole, there was a faint feeling of separateness or nationality among the Afghans, the Hindus and the Mughals.

The credit of successfully fighting away the Mughals goes to Sher Shah who did this with a view to establishing Afghan sovereignty in India. In the words of Ishwari Prasad, Sher Shah "had long set before himself the task of uniting the Afghans for expulsion of the Mughals. This he pursued with a cool and calculating patience, looking neither to the right nor to the left, always watchful, always cautious, never resting" (Prasad, 59). The Afghans were able to deny the throne of Delhi to Humayun for about 14 years (and not 15 years as generally assumed; because the Second Battle of Panipat was actually not a fight between the Mughals and the Afghans, but between the Mughals and the Hindu force commanded by Himu, the King of Delhi). Humayun regained the throne of Delhi in 1555 from the Afghans. In February of that year, Humayun, occupying the fort of Rohtas which Sher Shah built as a bulwark against Mughal invasion, reached Lahore and from there reached Jullundur via Haryana. At Machhiwara (in modern Ludhiana) not far from Sutlej, the Mughal and the Afghan forces met in an engagement. Tatar Khan Kashi, the Afghan commander had 50,000 horses which was numerically far superiror than the Mughal strength. "But they [The Afghans – SKS] were kept at bay by the Mughal archers till night-fall. Unfortunately a fire broke out in a large village of thatched houses and exposed the Afghan army completely. The Mughal archers took full advantage of it and plied them with showers of arrows till they broke and fled leaving their elephants and property to the Mughal" (Tripathi, 167). The battle of Machhiwara is the last great Afghan-Mughal conflict. After this, the main force of the Afghan dwindled.

After the battle of Machhiwara, Humayun proceeded towards Sirhind where Sikandar Lodi opposed him with a force of 80,000 strong. On June 22, 1555, the main battle of Sirhind was fought. In the preliminary stage of the battle, the Afghans seemed to be lucky to win but in the end the Afghans had to give way. The battle of Sirhind is remarkable, it may be added, in the sense that in this battle " 'on both sides humanity and gentleness were protected, so that the bodies of those who had sacrificed their lives were reverently made over to their friends' " (Tripathi, 168). However, after the battle of Sirhind, the regaining of the throne of Delhi was only a matter of days to Humayun, and after this the greatest battle the Mughals had to wage was not with the Afghan force, properly, but with the Hindu force.

II

(The Hindu-Mughal Conflicts)

Historians have so far done scant justice to the struggle of the Hindus for revival. India was not lost by the Hindus in 712 A.D. (Islam spread its net in Europe almost simultaneously, *i.e.*, at the beginning of the 8th century. But its victorious march under the command of Abdul Rahman was halted by Charles Martel in 732 in the battle of Tours or Poitiers). Ever since that time, the Hindus were active in repulsing the invasions of the Muslims from time to time, though not in an organized way, excepting in the battle of Und (1008) in which the Kings of Ujjain, Gwalior, Kalanjar, Kanauj, Delhi and Ajmer joined Anandapal against Sultan Mahmud. The extent of Hindu unity and sacrifice in this battle can be gauzed when we learn that even "The women from different parts of the country sold their jewels and sent the money for the war against the invader" (Sastri, 1986, 335). Yet Anandapal sustained a defeat which put an end to the Hindu Shahi. During the slave dynasty (1206–1290) and the House of Khalji (1290–1321), The Hindus retained the major portion of the sub-continental India under their control. "Even within the Empire [of Balban – SKS] Hindu chiefs remained in 'turbulent vigour' in the Doab, Malwa and Gujrat. All the rest of India continued to be ruled by numerous Hindu Kings ...." (Sastri, 1986, 349).

From the very beginning the Mughals were intent upon eliminating the Hindus from the Indian sub-continent. In 1398, Tamerlane invaded India to teach the Muslims of India, who were, he supposed, conniving at idolatry, a gruesome lesson. "At the cruel ruler's order, 100,000 prisoners were put to death. To intimidate the Hindus, Tamerlane has [*sic*] almost all the inhabitants of the conquered regions killed, and pyramids built with their skulls" (Agibalova, 177-78). Powell-Price says that most of the 100,000 prisoners were Hindus and that Tamerlane got them killed fearing they "might prove dangerous" (Powell-Price, 176). But, when the Mughals first tried to enter into India, it was not the Hindus but the Indianized Muslims (the slave Sultans, the Khalji Kings and The Tughlaq Kings) who put up resistances. Ghiyas-ud-din Balban repulsed an attack by Mangu, a Mongol, on Sindh. During The Khalji ruler, Ghazi Malik "repelled several invasions of Mongols" (Sastri, 357). One of the causes of Muhammad-bin-Tughluq's transfering the capital from Delhi to Devagiri was the threat of Mongol or Mughal invasions. Taimur

(Tamerlane), the Turk and a forebear of Babur, invaded India in 1398. Firuz Tughluq put up a resistance to Taimur (= 'The earth-shaker'). Ibrahim, the last Lodi King of Delhi, fought against Babur in the first battle of Panipat on 21st April, 1526, and sacrificed his life to save the independence of the country.

It was the first battle of Panipat in which, for the first time, the Hindus came forward to fight against the Mughals. In this battle Raja Vikramajit of Gwalior fought side by side with Ibrahim Lodi against Babur, the Mughal, and sacrificed his life, as did his about sixteen thousand soldiers. The first battle of Panipat stands out in the military history of India as the first battle in which the united Hindu and native Muslim (Afghan) forces made a common bloc against the Mughals.

After Panipat Babur came into direct conflicts with the Hindus. Rana Sanga, the ruler of Mewar, "was desirous of establishing Hindu rule in the country" (Mehta, 99). The dream of the Hindus of establishing Hindu supremacy was not new then. Even during the time of the last Khalji ruler, Nasir-ud-din Khusru, a Hindu convert, a "degenerate Hindu *raj* was established" (Sastri, 357). However, after Panipat, Babur became engaged in a battle with the old Rana Sanga (who had only one eye, one leg, one arm and had eighty scars of wounds of battles on his body). The Mughals and the Hindus met at the village of Khanwa, about 50 miles north-west of Agra, on 16 March, 1527. Before the battle, Babur, who was like Qutbuddin a *qalandar* or mendicant, "called in the aid of religion. He proclaimed a holy war, *jihad*. He assembled his troops and before them foreswore wine [afterwards he took wine moderately – SKS], breaking his jewelled wine cups and pouring out the stores of liquor. He made his soldiers swear on the *Koran* to fight for him" (Sastri, 445). This is a glaring instance of fanaticism; never before this was religion used in battles in India. True, proselytising to Islam and Hindu-Muslim conflicts were there, but the proselytising was done on good terms and the Hindu-Muslim conflicts were not there purely for religious reasons. For instance, in spite of some of his suppressing measures against the Hindus, Ala-ud-din Khilji followed "a purely secular state policy" (Sastri, 356). The Hindu-Muslim differences so far were mainly due to political reasons, and not so much due to religious differences. But Babur was avowedly an iconoclast and a fanatic at that. Babur's fanaticism is evident from the following verses of his :

> For the love of Faith I became
> a wanderer in the desert,

I became the antagonist of the
Pagans and Hindus
I strove to make myself
a martyr; —
Thanks to the Almighty God
who has made me a Ghazi.

(*Edwardes*, 125).

(Compare: "Destroy everything of the vanquished and if you like marry the women.", 'Deuteronomy', 21, *The Bible*). Therefore, we can, perhaps, say that Babur's declaration of a *jihad* was the first instance of overt communal frenzy in India.

To return to Hindu-Mughal conflicts. In spite of his victory at Khanwa (1527), "Babur did not dare to enter the heart of the Rajput territories; Chittor was defended heavily by the lieutenants of Rana Sanga, who set up his abode in the nearly hills with a vow not to enter the town without avenging his defeat suffered at the hands of Babur" (Mehta, 103, f.n.). H. Goetz writes that even after the battle of Khanwa, "No amiable relations were expected to develop under the then existing circumstances as the Rajputs looked down, with all their racial, pride of 'descendents of the gods' (Suryavamsis and Somavamsis), upon the abominable Turks" (Gupta, 125). The next battle of Babur was also with the Hindus. Medini Rao, the Rajput chief of Chanderi, fought besides Rana Sanga in the battle of Khanwa. After Khanwa Babur beseiged the fort of Chanderi. Rana Sanga was heavily wounded at Khanwa, but yet, "When he heard of the siege of Chanderi by Babur, he directed his lieutenants to take him to the place with an army to help Medini Rao. As luck would have it, he died en route to Chanderi a couple of days before the fort was conquered by Babur" (Mehta, 103, f.n.). Babur occupied Chanderi on January 29, 1528. "His soldiers had nevertheless to pass through a blood-bath as the defenders of the fort performed the ghastly rite of *jauhar* in the true Rajput spirit; they killed their women and children, put on the saffron-coloured garments and fell upon the enemy like hawks. They wrecked terrible vengeance upon the Mughal army before laying down their lives" (Mehta, 104).

After Babur, Humayun came into conflicts with the Hindu forces. Immediately after his accession, Humayun sent an expedition to the Hindu province of Kalinjar (in Bundekhand), perhaps because he thought, its Hindu *raja* was getting into a league with the Afghans of

Bihar, for a march against the Mughals. Humayun's army besieged the fort of Kalinjar for about six months without any avail. Ultimately a peace-treaty was concluded on the *raja's* nominal submission to Humayun. "Humayun hailed it a great victory but, as a matter of fact, the *raja* could not be beäten, and the incident exposed the weakness of the Mughal army" (Mehta, 111-112).

III

(The Hindu-Afghan Conflicts)

The Hindu-Afghan conflict was not a new phenomenon during the second Afghan dynasty, as even during the time of the Lodis, there occurred several Hindu-Afghan conflicts. For instance, during the reign of Sikandar Shah Lodi, the Hindu land-lords of Jaunpur gathered an army of 100,000 strong and rebelled. Sikandar Lodi picked up quarrels with the Hindu provinces of Gwalior and Utgir. Both Man Singh of Gwalior and Dungar of Utgir were defeated by Sikandar Lodi. However, as we are principally concerned with the time of Himu, let us confine our survey within the period of the second Afghan (Sur dynasty).

The first Hindu-Aghan conflict of importance occurred during the time of Sher Shah. In 1543, Sher Shah falsely accused Rai Puran Mall of Raisen of maltreating some Muslim citizens, and to punish Puran Mall, besieged Raisen. The Rajputs gave a tough resistance but in the end submitted to Sher Shah who gave them word that the lives of the Rajputs would be protected. But some fanatic Muslims pursuaded Sher Shah to break his promise. Sher Shah did so and, as Abbas writes in *Tarikh-i-Sher Shahi*, a general massacre of Hindus was done. "This victory encouraged Sher Shah to liquidate other Hindu principalities of northern India one by one" (Mehta, 126).

In the battle of Raisen a good number of Afghans were killed by the Hindus. Probably for this Sher Shah now turned his hawk's eyes towards Jodhpur, the capital of Marwar. Sher Shah sowed dissensions in the ranks and files of Jodhpur and principally by his cunning captured Jodhpur. But Maldeo, the ruler of Marwar, soon after recovered Jodhpur (in July, 1545), after the death of Sher Shah. G.B. Malleson writes : ".... Maldeo Singh had given to the great Sher Shah more trouble in the field than had any of his opponents" (Hunter, 74). However, after the fall of Jodhpur, many rulers of the states of Rajasthan, including Rana Uday Singh, submitted to Sher Shah. After this Sher Shah laid siege to the fort of Kalinjar in Bundelkhand which was then ruled by Raja Kirat Singh. Sher Shah died of an explosion during this siege, but before his death the fastness of Kalinjar was captured by the Afghans.

After Sher Shah, his son Jalal Khan ascended the throne on 26 May, 1545, assuming the title of Islam Shah, and killed the Raja of Kalinjar and seventy others who were taken prisoners to the capital. Islam Shah next came into conflict with the Rana of Udaipur who gave refuge to Khawas Khan who fled from Islam Shah. Islam Shah requested the Rana for the repatriation of Khawas Khan, but the Rana replied : " 'How can I throw into fetters a man who has sought my protection? As long as I have breath in my body I can never be guilty of such baseness' " (Tripathi, 146). Islam pursuaded Khawas Khan to come to him on the terms of amnesty and "appealed to his patriotism and religious insticts to come and lead a *holy war* against the Rana of Udaipur" (*italics* mine) (*ibid.*). Perhaps this is the second *Jihad* of the Muslims (Afghan) against the Hindus. Years after, the next great Hindu-Afghan engagement occurred on 14th January, 1761, in the battle-field of Panipat (the third battle of Panipat) where Shuja-ud-daulah completely defeated the Marathas led by Viswas Rao and the Bhau.

But in spite of these conflicts between the Hindus and the Afghans and in spite of Islam Shah's "holy war" against the Rana of Udaipur, and Sher Shah's several anti-Hindu measures, the relation between the Hindus and the Afghans generally remained healthy and peaceful. This was so because the two communities lived for a long time together, and also because a bond of affinity between the two communities was created by the messages of tolerance propagated by both Hindu and Muslim saints and great souls, during the previous and present centuries. A picture of the favourable condition for the Hindus during the second Afghan dynasty can be had from what Muhammad Farmuli once said to Islam Shah: " 'O, my liege! two nights I dreamt that three bags descended from heaven, one containing ashes, another gold and the third papers. The ashes fell upon the head of the troops, the gold upon the houses of the Hindus, and the papers fell to the lot of the treasury!' " (Tripathi, 153).

IV

(Conflicts Between the Hindu-Afghan and the Mughal Forces)

The Afghans and the Hindus fought against the Mughals not only as insolated forces, but also, at times, unitedly. This was so because the Afghans were in course of time, so to say, naturalised, unlike the Mughals. Jawaharlal Nehru is quite right when he says that the "*Afghans might well be considered a border Indian group, hardly strangers to India" but the Mughals were outsiders and strangers to India*" (italics mine) (Nehru, 241). We have already seen how the Hindus and the Afghans made a united bloc against the Mughals in the first battle of Panipat (1526). In this battle Ibrahim Lodi, son of Sikandar Lodi, fought hand in hand with Raja Vikramajit of Gwalior, and both became martyrs. In the next battle of Babur (battle of Khanwa, 1527) also the Hindus and the native Muslims (Afghans) fought shoulder to shoulder. In spite of Babur's declaration of a *jihad* against the 'pagans' and in spite of his all out effort "to arouse the Muslims to make a united effort against the Rana" (Tripathi, 39). The native Muslims (Afghans) fought against the Mughal foreigners. According to James Tod, Babur exhibited utter "*frenzy of religion* in " 'this holy war' " (*infra*). To impress his followers, Babur ceased to cut bear and assured the soldiers of waiving the levy of Temgha (stamp-tax) from them if he won the battle of Panipat (Tod, 243-44).

After Babur, Humayun once experienced a two-pronged attack of the Hindus and the native Muslims (Afghans). Even during the time of Humayun's ascension, "the Mughals were still treated as foreigners; and were hated and despised by the Indians, both Hindus as well as Muslims" (Mehta, 109). The historic fort of Kalinjar situated on an isloated rock on the Vindhyas was attacked by Humayun, seven or eight months after his ascension. Raja Pratap Rudra of Kalinjar also declared war on the Mughals. "Hardly had the siege continued for a month when came the most disquieting news that Mahmud Lodi, brother of Ibrahim Lodi, had captured Jaunpur and the Mughal officers had been compelled to retreat. Humayun, therefore, came to some ambiguous terms with Raja Pratap Rudra and hurried up towards Chunar" (Tripathi, 69). These and such others are instances of conflicts between the Hindus and the Afghans on the one hand and the Mughals on the other.

V

(The Social Status of the Hindus and the Possibility of Hindu Revival)

A

(The Social Status of the Hindus)

This is a very complicated and not-yet-fully-explored area of medieval Indian history. Therefore we should be very cautious about sweeping comments, because sometimes these are opinionated and prejudiced. However, it may generally be admitted that the Hindus constituted the lowest rung of the society. They served the Afghans and the Mughals in their soldiery, for livelihood. The *jiziya* (tax imposed upon non-Muslims for living in a Muslim State) was imposed by both the Mughals and the Afghans. (Sometimes this tax was condoned in the case of Brahmins because of their higher status in the Hindu society.) True, Sher Shah as well as some other Muslim sovereigns sometimes launched attacks on Hindu States, but in most of the cases, all these were inspired by political motives and not religious ones. K.A. Nilakanta Sastri and G. Srinivasachari rightly say that Sher Shah "never oppressed the Hindu subjects" (Sastri, 455). Not only the Sur Kings, but the Khalji rulers also were generally above bigotry. For instance, Ala-ud-din Khilji planned to float a new religion as a prototype of Akbar's Din-i-Ilahi. Before the coming of the Mughals, the native Muslims recruited Hindu soldiers in their army. "Even Mahmud Ghazni maintained a large corps of Hindu horse. His son Masud wanted his officers to respect the susceptibilities of Hindu soldiers. Tilak, a Hindu barbar's son was appointed to suppress the rebellion of (the Muslim) Ahmed Nialtigin. This shows that the process of assimilation between the Turks [and other native Muslims, but not the Mughals – SKS] and Indians [Hindus – SKS] began very early." (Sastri, 377). Muslim Kings and Emperors sometimes conferred high titles on Hindu allies and subjects. Humayun, for instance, before his defeat at the hands of Sher Shah, conferred on Baharma the high title of Raja of Ambar (Hunter, 73).

There were instances of very generous and catholic Muslim (generally non-Turkish) rulers. Muhammad Adil Shah of Bijapur, like Zainal Abedin of Kashmir and Akbar the great (called Jagatguru by the Emperor's Hindu subjects), was very generous to the Hindus, and so "was called 'Jagatguru' by his Muslim subjects for his patronage of Hindus in the States" (Sarkar and Datta, vol. I, 6). The Hindu-Muslim rapport was enhanced by Sufism whose "sense of asceticism is alien to the spirit of Islam" (Q' Leary, 182) but which was born, and found a favourable ground, in India. Writes Augustus: "Sufism when transplanted to India, found in the minds of the native thinkers a fruitful soil in which it spread wide and developed, for the *brahmanas* were superior to Muhammadans in disciplined thought as the latter were to the *brahmanas* in depth of feeling and in the passion of mystical enthusiasm" (Augustus, 28). Sufism flourished in India due to the Muslim saints as well as Hindu saints and philosophers, such as Ramananda, Vallabha, Chaitanya, Kabir and Nanak. Vallabha (1473-1531), founder of *Suddhadvaita* sect preached the philosophy of love during the time of Humayun and Akbar, near Allahabad.

The Hindus sometimes showed interest in Muslim theology. The first translation of the Quran in an Indian language was done not by a Muslim but by a Gujrati Hindu whom the Muslims affectionately called Lal Muhammad. During the period under discussion, we find such great Muslim mystics as Shaikh Budh, the holy man of Bihar (whom Sher Shah held in high esteem) and Shaikh 'Alai who professed the religion of Mehdi at Biyana. These Sufis were influenced also by Hindu Yoga philosophy. In some cultural areas the Muslims were so much influenced by the Indian cultural heritage that they began to believe even in Indian superstitions (*Punjab Univ. Research Bulletin, Arts*, vol. XIX, No. 1, April, 1988, pp. 137-146). We have also seen instances of very moving personal friendships between Hindus and Muslims, for example that between Mahbub, the Commander of Alaud-din and Ratansi. (Waley, 165-16). Again, it is not always true to say that only the Muslims sometimes ill-treated the Hindus, but on the contrary, the Hindus also ill-treated Muslims. Jauher, for instance, in his *Tezkerah al Vakiat*, writes: "When arrived in the pergunnah, I found that it had been the custom of the Afghan farmers to give their wives or children in pledge to the *Hindu* bankers for money advanced on account of the collections; ...." (Jauher, 121).

It is not true that the Hindus and for that matter the Hindu culture were not at all attended to by Muslim sovereigns. Even as late as in the reign of Shahjahan we find that the Muslim Emperor enjoyed the companions of the Hindu intellectuals. For example, in the *Padshahnamah* "we get interesting references to the Emperor's [Shahjahan's – SKS] patronage of Hindu poets, musicians, artists and intellectual prodigies" (Ojha, 109). Examples of these are not few in number. It is curious to note that even Aurangzeb honoured his staunchest enemy Shivaji with the title of Raja (King) as we learn from the former's letter to the latter, dated 24 February, 1668 (Kincaid, 225). Of course, some historians opine that these are, probably, examples of exceptions rather those of the general policies adopted by the Muslim sovereigns.

The cultural and sentimental fusion of the two communities shed its influence on the birth and growth of the Urdu language and literature as well as on the metamorphosis of the Dingal (डिंगल) language and literature. Urdu grew out of the fusion of Arabic and Persian of the Muslims and the Khadi Boli of the Hindus (of modern Uttar Pradesh). But according to N.S. Gorekar, Urdu was born out of the marriage between Hariani and Persian. However, Urdu, or, as Amir Khusru called it, Dehlavi, "as a language is the practical outcome of the Hindu-Muslim entente, which has been established by the fact that a genuine spirit of unity, cordiality and self-sacrifice induced both Hindus and Muslims to forego their respective languages and to adopt as their own a language essentially Indian in origin but fully nourished and developed on foreign resources" (Roychoudhury, 155). The influence of Arabic and Persian was also very much felt in the Dingal language and literature: " डिंगल रचनाओं में अरबी-फारसी शब्दों का बाहुल्य जितना उतरमुगल काल में प्रण्त है, उतना प्रारभ्भिक काल में नहीं।" (सारस्वत, ५४). M.L. Roychoudhury, in his *The State and Religion in Mughal India*, extensively showed the cultural association between the Hindus and the Muslims during the medieval India. In the sphere of literature, for example, writes Roychoudhury, "The Muslims [on the other hand – SKS], introduced their books with the names of the Hindu gods. To mention a few of them: – " 'Abdur Rahim began his Madanastaka with the name of Ganesa. Ahamad 'llah opend his Nayikabheda with Sri. Ramji Sahaya; as he proceeded, he adopted Atha Saraswati Stuti and Ganesa Ki Stuti." Ya'qub Khan in his Rasabhusana invoked blessings not only of Sri Ganesa but also of a series of Hindu gods and goddesses – Saraswati, Krisna, Sri Radha, and Sri Sankara. "Gulam Nabi in his Ananga Darpana used the name of Sri Ganesa at the beginning. "Azam Khan began his Sringar Darpana after offering obeisance to the Hindu saint Ramanuja" (Roychoudhury, 275-76). All these were not new phenomena in Mughal period; they gradually took roots in the pre-Mughal period. We have only taken here instances from the times of the Mughal administration.

According to Khaliq Ahmed Nizami, "Most of the Turks who had established the Sultanate of Delhi were, no doubt, neophytes but they were singularly free from all religious bigotry or fanaticism. If there was any element of exclusive thinking, its source was racial, not religious ...... [For example – SKS] Shihab-u'd-din continued the figures of the goddess Lakshmi on his gold coins .... Qutb-u'd-din Aibek allowed the Rajput Princes to rule over Delhi, Ajmer and

Gwalior even after the conquest of those regions. The Turkish nobles did not hesitate in entering into alliances with the Hindu chieftains" (Nizami, 316). After that, we see that some of the Mughal rulers were very sympathetic to the Hindu sentiment. In 1620, Francoys Pelsaert visited India as a Dutch factor and remained here for about seven years. In his book *Remonstrantee,* his "remarks about the district courts and the prohibition of slaughter of cows are interesting. He attributes this prohibition to a regard on the part of the government of Hindu sentiment, ..." (Saksena, xxi-xxii). This attitude was to be found both during the Mughal period and during the pre-Mughal period.

But all was not well for the Hindus during the Afghan and Mughal periods. It cannot be denied that at the beginning of their coming to India, the Timurids were avowedly anti-Hindu in attitude. "It is said Timur invaded India on the pretext that the Turkish Sultans were unduly tolerant towards Hindus" (Sastri, 377). Waley speaks of "all the atrocities and excesses proclaimed by the earliest Musulanman emperors of India" (Waley, 252). The Hindus were never treated as on a par with the Muslims. P. Kohli is not all amiss when he says that "Excluding Akbar all the Mohammedan rulers were anti-Hindu in their views. The Muslim rule hampered on the whole the cultural growth of the Hindus" (Kohli, 212). The Muhammedans could not identify themselves with the natives. Augustus writes: "The Muhammedans however were too alien in faith and character for their amalgamation with the earlier settlers to have been possible, except in cases where these had previously become converts to Islam." (Augustus, 17). In a few cases, even the Afghan rulers were no better than the Mughal ones. Sikandar Lodi, formerly known as Nizam Khan, the son of a daughter of a Hindu goldsmith by Bahlul Lodi, the King of Delhi, in spite of his intellectual accomplishments (he compiled a compendium of medicine based on Arabic and Sanskrit sources), was a Hindu-iconoclast (Powell-Price, 188). Even before that, we can recount, the ruthless and ceaseless plunders of Mahmud of Ghazni caused "aversion of the Hindus towards all Muslims" (Mishra, 225). The Hindus certainly grudged their obligation of paying the *jiziya* tax. They also could not bear with the forceful proselytising to Islam. The Hindus accepted the practice of the Muslims of marrying Hindu wives, but Muslims could not allow the Hindus to marry Muslim girls. Economically also the Hindus were not favoured with the benefits that the Muslims enjoyed. Therefore, "the bulk of the population in the country were never truly reconciled to the rule of the Sultanate" (*ibid.*). Nevertheless, the communal tension had not been surfacing so much during the Sultanate and the Afghan periods, as it was during the Mughal period. The Mughal or later Turkish attitude towards the Hindus can be gleaned from Taimur's grudging the Sultans of Delhi for their catholic attitude shown towards the Hindus. As against the affability of the Afghan rulers, some of the Taimuride rulers, overly enthusiastic to their own religion as they were, exhaled the first miasma of fundamentalism that afterwards showed its pernicious head from time to time, even as lately as in recent times. On the other hand, the causes of Hindu fundamentalism are to be sought elsewhere.

According to Arnold Toynbee, "..... Islam, like the other two religions of the Judaic family, is exclusive-minded and intolerant by comparison with the religions and philosophies of Indian origin" (*infra*). In this regard, he temptingly compares Ashoka and pre-Indianized Akbar: "Though Akbar, like Ashoka, renounced war on animals, he did not also make Ashoka's renunciation of war against human beings ...... [Yet – SKS] we may guess that Ashoka would still have done what he did do if the accident of birth had put him in Akbar's place instead of his own" (Toynbee, 19). Toynbee continues: "Intolerance is common to Christianity, Islam, Judaism and Zoroastrianism, ..." (Toynbee, 57). James Tod is also exasperated at the kind of people that the Mughals were. He calls these people "barbarous, bigotted and exasperated foes" (Tod, xiv). It is really strange to think that even Akbar "was long ranked with Shahabuddin, Alla [Alauddin Khilji – SKS] and other instruments of destruction, and with every just claim; and, like those, he constructed a Mumba [pulpit for the leader of congregated Muslims for prayers – SKS] for the Koran from altars of Ekling" (Tod, xiii). This inhuman attitude of Akbar is attested by Will Durant when he says that "...... by a series of ruthless wars he [Akbar – SKS] made himself ruler of all Hindustan except for the little Rajput Kingdom of Mewar" (Durant, 465). Sarkar and Datta are also of the opinion that the arrival of the Mughals in India was a new condition for the "prolongation of medievalism" (*infra*) and that the "Religious persecution and fanatism took the place of religious toleration" (Sarkar and Datta, 8-9). In the eyes of its followers [Islam's followers – SKS], the land [of India – SKS] was full of idols; the various sects of Brahmanism, Buddhism and Jainism were equally abominable to the worshippers of Allah, the One God.

The fanatical Moslems preferred to kill the infidel in battle or butcher him in the subsequent pursuit; for the survivors there were two alternatives : acceptance of the teachings of the Koran, or payment of crushing taxation. Such a fanatic was Mahmud of Ghazni, whom we have seen controlling Persia from his Afghan Court" (Weech, 325) and "*With him [Mahmud of Ghazni – SKS] begins the long enmity between Moslem and Hindu which has lasted to the present day*" (Weech, 326) (emphasis added). Qutbuddin's "personal pleasure and religious duty demanded the shedding of infidel blood" (*op. cit.*, 327). This anti-Hindu attitude of the invading Muslims subsided during the time of Akbar, only to raise its ugly head afterwards in the reign of Aurangzeb. H. Goetz writes that this "anti-Rajput or anti-Hindu attitude under Aurangzeb developed into a conscious anti-Hindu policy" (Gupta, 134). But, let us recant it once over that this anti-Hindu attitude had its roots well before the coming of the Mughals.

The Hindus are also sometimes accused of bigotry and fanaticism. Ferista, for instance, writes : "The infidels of Vijoynagar, who for many years had been wishing such an event, left no cruelty unpractised; they insulted the honour of the Musalman women, destroyed the mosques, and did not even respect the sacred Quran" (Prasad, 131).

However, India is not to be despised on account of her religious intolerance in those days, for even in Europe religious toleration was not in sight till Henry IV (or Henry of Navarre) issued the Edict of Nantes in 1598. Side by side with the Muslim iconoclastic aggression (compare: "In the land that you are taking, destroy the places where the people worship their gods ...... Tear down their altars .... chop down their idols .....", 'Deuteronomy', 12, *The Bible*), we find the Muslim attitude of coming closer to the Hindu society and Hindu sentiment. Thus, the Muslims, for example, frequently married Hindu wives, though the Hindus did not reciprocate such cementing attitude on the part of the Muslims (maybe, because the Muslims did not allow their daughters to marry Hindus, and also because the Hindus regarded such marriages as morganetic). Of course, in most of the cases, the Muslims married Hindu wives forcefully. For example, Malik Muhammad Jaisi (1464-1542) in his poem 'पदमावत' narrated how Ala-ud-din Khalji forcibly married पदमावती! Though the poem was composed on the wings of poesy, yet it contains historical truth. According to Jaisi, Ala-ud-din was beside himself at the nymph-like beauty of Padmavati, and to possess her, he arrested and took away her husband Ratnasen in chains to Delhi. "बादशाह को एक ही शर्त थी — पदमावती को देकर छुटकारा सम्भव है। रतनसेन इस पर कैसे सहमत हो सकता था। उसे अन्धकूप में डाल दिया गया।" (श्रीवास्तव, 23).

It should be noted here that the social history of medieval India has not yet been well studied by historians. The study of the social history of medieval India was started by W.H. Moreland in the first quarter of this century, and since then, according to Satish Chandra, we have only "limited understanding of social history during the period" (*The Indian Historical Review, 268*) (The present author's next endeavour will be to enter into this obscure area of medieval Indian history). Nevertheless, we can, perhaps, for the time being, agree with G.B. Malleson who writes that "According to all concurrent testimony, the condition of the Hindu population, who constituted seven-eighth of the entire population of the provinces subject to Muhammedan rule, was one of contentment" (Hunter, 74).

B

(*The Possibility of Hindu Revival*)

Himu's assuming the title of Vikramaditya and his becoming an independent King of Delhi should not be viewed as an isolated event. If we study Indian history from the time when the Muslims first began to rule India, to the period we are concerned with here, very closely, we will find that there have been continuous attempts on the part of the Hindus to shake off foreign yoke and revive their past glory and independence. During the period, though the Hindus numerically dominated India, yet it was not possible for them to regain their lost political supremacy because the major portion of India was dominated and ruled by the Muslims, native and foreign (Mughal); and also because there was no consciousness among the Hindus of their nationality. Nevertheless, the Hindus ruled at least some provinces of the country as we have seen in Chapter II. Perhaps, if the numerically overwhelming Hindu once stood unitedly, they could throw overboard the domination of the Muslims and retrieve their lost independence.

It is not true that the Hindus lost India to the Muslims in 712 when Raja Dahir was defeated by Muhammed-bin-Kasim in Sind, or in 1192 when Prithviraj Chauhan was defeated by Sultan Muhammad Ghori in the battle of Tarain. But, the Hindu strength had been constantly battered by incessant foreign invasions since 712, as a result of which the Hindu power in Northern India was gradually becoming weaker and weaker. Nevertheless, till the third battle of Panipat (1761), the Hindu forces tirelessly, calculatedly and constantly had been trying to regain India's lost independence. But all these were of no avail, primarily because such efforts were scattered and also because these did not receive the united support of the reticent Hindu mass soaked in the extremely tolerant Hindu philosophy of life. Nevertheless, Mr. Justice Mahadeo Govind Ranade is not all amiss when he, in consonance with Grant Duff, writes: "In the first place, it should be noted that the immediate predecessors of the British rulers of India were not the Mahomedans, as is too often taken for granted but they were the native [Hindu – SKS] rulers of the country, who had successfully thrown off the Mahomedan yoke" (Ranade, 2). It will be a long history to narrate the Hindu strength of yore. We can perhaps glean an idea of it from the valour of Laksmi-Karna or Lakshmanaraja of the Chedi clan, who set an instance of Hindu strength "By unceasing military activity [in the eleventh century – SKS] Laksmi-Karna extended his dominions from Western Bengal to the borders of Gujarat" (Ray, 1215). Hindu martial spirit declined, says H.C. Ray, due mainly to the Hindu's caste system and the cult of *Ahimsa*. These made the Hindus too weak to cope with the "barbarian conquerors" (Marx, 30) who were not till then what the poet, John Dryden, called "a glorious Race" (Mahajan, 145).

The history of India from 712 to 1761 is not a history of Muslim attacks on the Hindus only; during the period, the Hindus also made several attacks on the Muslims. We know that the Hindu Sahia dynasty was very strong and dominated all the regions around Kabul which probably was the capital. Trilochanapal, a later King of this dyanasty, came into conflict with the "Turushka" ruler "Hammira" (Amir Muhammad of Ghazni). King Sangramaraja helped Trilochanapala, but the latter was defeated (Mishra, 7). Though Taimur in 1398 dealt a heavy blow to Delhi and then returned, "Moslem power had been weakened and renewed Hindu resistance made possible" (Weech, 328). Simultaneously, "In the south the Hindus rallied and checked the further progress of Islam" (Weech, 328). However, let us see very briefly how far the Hindus could attack the Muslims, and preserve their domination over India. During the time of Subuktigin, Jaipal marched upon Ghazni, twice – once in 979, and again in 988, being supported by the strength of Ajmer and

Kanauj. Subuktigin was succeeded by Mahmud of Ghazni who looted India for seventeen times. During his second invasion Jaipal was reduced to eat his humble pie. Jaipal emolated himself into fire and Anandapal ascended the thone. At this time Mahmud intended an attack on Multan, and so its ruler, Abul Fath Daud sought the help of Anandapal. This made Mahmud irate and he marched against Anandapal, reduced him, to humbleness and threw his son, Sukhapal, into prison, for life. "Now the Hindu Kings who had so long been indifferent realized the danger and strengthened Anandapal's defence. In A.D. 1008 the Kings of Ujjain, Gwalior, Kalinjar, Kanauj and possibly also Delhi and Ajmere, marched with their troops to the Punjab to fight against Mahmud and his army. The women from different parts of the country sold their jewels and sent the money for the war against the invader" (Sastri, 334-35). Unfortunately for the Indians, the elephant of Anandapal ran away, being wounded, from the battle-field of Und, and the Hindus lost the day. This war shows us two important things: one, the conflicts between the Indians and the foreigners were not always on communal lines; for instance Mahmud's army consisted of a large number of Hindu soldiers; and two, there was a faint consciousness of nationality among the Indians.

The Chalukyas of Gujrat and Kathiawad played a great role in keeping the foreign Muslims away from India. The Gurjara Pratihars also contributed to the defence of the country against Muslim aggressions. For instance, Nagabhatta I pushed back the aggression of the Arabs. But the contributions of the Chalukya Kings in this regard is of more importance. In 1176, Muhammad Ghori was miserably defeated at the hands of the Chalukya (Hindu) King Bhima II, when Ghori was attacking Gujrat. Again, in 1191, Prithviraj Chauhan confronted Muhammad Ghori in the battle of Tarain, and dealt a crushing defeat on him. In the eastern sector also there was a Hindu resistance. Zamindar Ganesh seized power and became an independent ruler of Bengal, during the time of Saifuddin Hamza Shah who succeeded Giasuddin Azam Shah, the ruler of Bengal. Before that, in the southern part of India, five sons of Sangama founded the Vijoynagar empire in 1336 on the bank of the river Tungabhadra. This was another instance of Hindu revivalism. Vijoynagar continued to exist till it was erdicated by the Muslims in the battle of Talicot in 1565. Adolf Waley writes: "In spite of their subjugation by Ala-ud-din Khilji, the spirit of their people [of Vijoynagar, the Hindu Kingdom of Mysore – SKS] had never been broken and the

Tamils of the Carnatic, the Malayahis of Malabar, the Kanarese of Mysore and the Telegus of Warrangal alike bided their time only until leaders should arise in their midst to help them to throw off the hated yoke of the Musulman" (Waley, 196). In 1526, Babur destroyed the Sultanate of Delhi but the Hindu power was yet unaffected. The Hindu power was dealt with a heavy blow on in the battle of Khanwa (1527). Before that Rana Sanga had been dreaming of Hindu revival. Augustus writes : "Rana Sanka [Rana Sanga – SKS] in allying with Babur [before the first battle of Panipat – SKS], had intended to make every occasion subservient to the establishment in power and independence of his own people, at the expense of the mutually hostile Muhammedans ... The day when they (the Rajput Hindus – SKS] were lords of India was indeed long past but men of the mould of Sanka and high-spirited comrades could neither forget nor forgo the time of their earlier supremacy" (Augustus, 45). After the first battle of Panipat (1526), Ibrahim Lodi's mother contrieved through the agency of one aimed to poison Babur who was providentially saved. As we saw above, Tripathi righty writes: "..... had he [Babur – SKS] been murdered 'nothing could have saved the Kingdom, which he was building up, and the Rajputs would have been supreme in Hindustan" (Tripathi, 39). Yes, though Babur defeated Sangram Singh in the battle of Khanwa, yet neither he nor Humayun could take away Mewar from the Rajputs. S.C. Sarkar and K.K. Datta write : "A study of the history of Mughal India as a whole shows that after Khanwah, the Rajputs retire only for the time being from the field of politics; they reappear once again after thirty years and make their influence felt for close upto two centuries. *Nor is the tide of Hindu revival completely checked for those thirty years, – since Sher Shah had to struggle with the Rajput States, and his descendents fell into the power of Himu who assumed the title of Vikramaditya*" (italics mine) (Sarkar and Datta, 24). Hindu resurgency was observed in Western India where "Sindh and Multan had freed themselves from imperial control after death of Sher Shah" (*op. cit*, 54). Niccolo Manucci at least once immuendoes to the possibility of Hindu resurgence: "Finding himself undisputed master of Hindustan, and loved by his people, he [Xira or Sher Shah – SKS] made war against the Rana, a Hindu King, assuming command of the army in person. But he was repulsed in such a fashion that if the Hindu King had pursued he would have become the lord of the whole country" (Manucci, 115). But this is only in line with the antic historian Livy who "is a model for the narrative of an event which never happened," as Isaac Disraeli in his essay "Of A History of Events which Have Not Happened" says (Disraeli, 430). Again, Uday Singh, Sangram Singh's son, fled away when Akbar attacked Chitor and Akbar annexed Chitor, the chief fastness of the Rajputs, but, yet the other part of Mewar was still ruled by Rana Pratap, the son of Uday Singh. Rana Pratap, was defeated by Akbar in 1576 in the battle of Haldighati (Gogunda, just north-west of Udaipur). The Rana died in 1597, after 21 years of hardship for the freedom of India from foreign (Mughal) domination. After his death, Amar Singh routed an attack on Mewar by Man Singh, the Cammander-in-Chief of Akbar, in 1599. Akbar annexed Gondwana from Rani Durgabati in 1564 after defeating the *Rani* in the battle of Gondwana. The *Rani* sacrificed her life for Hindu cause of independence. It may be mentioned here that during the time of Akbar, twelve zamindars of Bengal refused to acknowledge the suzerainty of Akbar, of whom a few were Hindu (Chand Ray, Kedar Roy and Pratapaditya), and they fought for the independence of the Hindus, though Sir Sarkar does not admit that they were patriots.

The Hindu spirit of independence continued to inspire upto the reign of Aurangzeb. Owing to his anti-Hindu policy, Aurangzeb had to face a number of Hindu uprisings. He had to suppress thrice the Jat rebellions, once the Bundella and once the Satnami rebellions. Aurangzeb's army was defeated by the Bundella chief Chhatrashal in 1671 and the Chhatrashal had been reigning independently in the Eastern Malwa. Aurangzeb had also to fight with the Sikhs — a branch of the Hindu community. But the strongest enemies of Aurangzeb were the Rajputs and the Marathas. Rajput Durga Das, and Marathi Shivaji, who dreamt of a Hindu Shahi, harassed Aurangzeb immensely. Shivaji wanted to found a great *Hindu Rastra* and actually he could carve out a moderate chunk of the Indian territory for this purpose. But this Hindu spirit of revivalism bore no fibre of hatred towards the other community. V.B. Kulkarni writes about Shivaji: "He saw with the clarity of a satesman the need for asserting the political independence of the Hindus as the only means of establishing a real community of interests between them and the Muslim minority." The successors of Shivaji went on even further. Bajirao I wanted to found a *Hindupada Padshahi* and with this end in view he united many of the Hindu *Rajas* and *zamindars* in a confederacy. But in the third battle of Panipat (January 14, 1761), Ahmed Shah Adbali dashed to the ground this dear dream of the Maratha Confederacy of establishing a *Hindupada*

Padshahi, when Abdali inflicted a crushing defeat on Sadashivrao Bhao.

This brief narrative may show us the fact that since the first Muslim incursion into India to the time of the coming of the British rule to India, the Hindus resorted to a long chain of rebellious efforts to jettison the Muslim domination and retrieve the lost independence of the Hindus — in short the Hindus had been striving for Hindu revivalism. It should be noted here that due to long cohabitation with the Afghans and to the catholic spirit of the religious preachers of the post-Sultanate period, the Hindus were not as much anti-Afghan as they were anti-Mughal. The Hindus well-nigh forgot their differences from the Afghan or native Muslims. But, when the Mughals (or Chaghtai Turks) gate-crashed into India with the first shibboleth of *jihad*, they once more became aware of their differences from the Muslim community of invaders, and also of their lost glory. Consequently, they became aware of the need of retrieving at least some parts of India where they could live independently, without having to obey willy-nilly the Muslim religious dictates on the *Dhimmis*, such as paying of *jiziya*, and without having to see their temples demolished by the invaders. This rebellious tendency of the Hindus was tampered only by the catholicity of Akbar, the great. But when Aurangzeb once again tried to revert India to the olden days of Babur, the Hindus immediately jumped on rebellion. However, it is not true that the Hindus were not aware of the incessant Muslim invasions and that they did not try to resist all these. To support our view, let us quote from C.V. Vaidya at some length: "That the Hindu Kingdoms in India were not alive to the danger and did not unite [during Mahmud's invasions – SKS] is not a fact, as we actually see in the history recorded by Mahomedans themselves. A new and dangerous religion had come to the frontiers of India long ago, *viz*. in Sind in 712 and the Hindus then, under the first Rajput warriors of Mewad and Sambhar, offered a most stubborn resistance to the Arabs and staged their onward march for ever. Three hundred years later came the Turks fired with the fanaticism of new proselytes and establishing themselves at Ghzni began to harass the Hindus and destroy their temples. Nay the Hindus had an experience of what was coming on, 60 years before, when Zabulistan was first taken by Yakub-i-Lais and his governor destroyed a famous Hindu temple at Sakhawand and Rai Kambu of Kabul was staggered at the sacrilege. The Hindu Kings were, therefore, alive to the danger from long experience and did thrice combine, brought large armies larger than those which Mahmud could oppose them, yet failed. The idea, therefore, that the Hindu Kings were oblivious of the peril and did not unite is entirely against the facts." (Vaidya, 111). Himu was only one of those Hindu Kings who were aware of the "peril" and rose to the occasion at his best. But, this revivalism did not die with Himu but continued to exist till the reign of Aurangzeb. Sarkar and Datta write: " The revived Hindu powers like the Marathas, the Rajputs, the Sikhs and the Jats tried to 'feed fat their ancient grudge' and made another bid for Hindu supremacy. Conscious of his failure and his approaching end, Aurangeb wrote to his son Azam : 'I came alone and am going alone. I have not done well to the country and the poeple, and of the future there is no hope'. " (Sarkar and Datt, 95). Hindu revivalism again showed its head during the middle of the eighteenth century. A.L. Srivastava writes: "The Maratha policy in Northern India during the years 1757–59 was extremely ambitious. Their dominion in Hindustan had grown out of an humble beginning and now their idea of *Hindupad Padshahi* embraced the whole of the country including the north-western *Subah* of the Punjab and the western-most province of Bengal" (Srivastava, 67). It may be added here that even in the relatively temperate reign of Shahjahan also we find Hindu rebellions, as that of Jagat Singh.

Therefore, Himu's assuming the title of Vikramaditya and his becoming an independent King of Delhi should not be viewed as an isolated event. We have earlier seen that even during the second Afghan dynasty, the Hindus were never treated by the Muslims as at par with them. Though Sher Shah's administrative policy was moderately secular, yet even he adopted some anti-Hindu measures, and sometimes showed attitude unfavourable to the Hindus. Even Islam Shah was not different from Sher Shah in this regard. The youthful Himu might have seen all these clearly, and as such might have developed a wish of seeing a Hindu Kingdom. But it was all only a wish, a dream, till when he rose to the highest rank of Adil Shah's army. He also found a favour of luck in Islam Shah's sympathy for him and in Adil Shah's being a worthless, happy-go-lucky and popinjay but luxuriant royal stamp, and Himu very efficiently utilized the opportunity.

We may conclude this section saying the possibility of Hindu revival was there during the time of Himu. It is perhaps true that if Himu could win the Second Battle of Panipat, Delhi and its surrounding areas in Northern India might continue to be ruled by the Hindus. Nonetheless, we should not forget that both the Afghans and the Mughals, in the inner regards of their hearts, nursed an amount of hatred for the Hindus, as so J.C. Powell-Price is, perhaps equally right when he writes that "Himu, had he won (the Second Battle of Panipat – SKS) would have been unlikely to have retained the loyalty of the Afghans who made up the great majority of his force, and the young Akbar would in time have returned to the assault" (Powell-Price, 247).

CHAPTER VI

An Assessment of Himu

An assessment of Himu will be amiss if we do not take into account his hereditary *locus standus*, the cause for which he fought till the end of his short life, and the great future which he might have been an heir to had he not been killed in the Second Battle of Panipat. It needs well a stretch of imagination to think how an ordinary huckster selling common salt in the winding streets of Rewari one day came to be the King of Delhi, and that too in a country dominated by people of an alien religious persuasion. Himu can be compared with Bahlul Lodi or Diocletus who rose from the status of a private soldier to that of a King; or with the "Slave Kings" of the Delhi Sultanate who rose to the penacle of authority and power by sheer dint of their merits. But Himu certainly stands out among them all since he achieved the unachieveable in spite of all sorts of hindrances. To speak about a few : physically, Himu was short in stature and thin in frame, and yet he became a Commander-in-Chief; he was a Hindu by religion, and yet he commanded an army with a majority of Muslim soldiers; and he served a Muslim master, but founded a Hindu Kingdom. Though small of frame, he was brave; though a weakling, he could sometimes be desperate; and though uninitiated in the science of logistics, he was a good commander. He was loyal and shrewd; exacting and calculating; a realist of the present and yet a dreamer of the future. He combined within himself the qualities of a good general, a worldly-wise counsellor, a skilful adiministrator, and an efficient empire-builder. In these regards he may, perhaps, be compared with Sher Shah and Akbar. And, perhaps, Himu was like the ideal man of Shakespeare – soldierly, scholarly (in the Elizabathan sense) and honest.

I

(*As a General*)

Himu first showed great skill as an administrator. The uncommon intelligence and excellent parts of this huckster must have impressed people who felt an urge to inform Islam Shah of these all, and the King appointed him an weighman. He discharged his duties so efficiently that within a very short period he became *Shahana-i-bazar* and then *Daroga-i-Chowki*. After Islam Shah, Adil Shah gave him some independent military operational charges, and he must have discharged his duties exemplarily well, for we know that afterwards he was bestowed heavier military responsibilities, and he proved his uncommon skill in all the 22 battles that he is said to have waged, and he was "everywhere victorious" (Abu-l-Fazl, 619). History can scarcely show examples of fits of this nature. In the medieval Indian history only Rana Sanga came close to Himu with eighteen battles won. He was a desparado in the battle-field, so much so that even Abu-l-Fazl praised his 'virile spirit' (Prasad, 229). But he must have combined skill, sagacity and bravado in himself, otherwise he could not win so many battles in a row.

Himu's task as the Commander-in-Chief of the Afghan army was very difficult and delicate. Firstly, he had to adjust himself with the capricious King. Secondly, he commanded an army which consisted mostly of Afghan Muslims, and he belonged to the Hindu community, the members of which held only the status of second-class citizens. Thirdly, even the (Hindu) Rajputs in his army grudged his leadership as he belonged to the low-rung *baniya* caste. In spite of all these difficulties and hindrances, Himu proved himself quite efficient and uncommon in all the spheres he had trodden, and so K.R. Quanungo very rightly writes: " 'No Hindu had been covered with so many glorious wounds on the field of battle except Maharana Sanga .... No Rajput wielded the sword so bravely against the foreign invaders as this humble Hindu of Rewari did on the battle-field of Panipat' " (Bharadwaj 88). Himu showed both mettle and equanimity. Mr. Bharadwaj writes: "He [Himu – SKS] defeated Junaid Khan, who was one of the deadliest rebels against Adil Shah. He showed great restraint which is expected of a military general. The foul language of Junaid Khan's general 'O, shopkeeper, why do you meddle with war? Return to your weights and scales' did not make Himu furious. On the other hand he remained alert, attacked him at a suitable time" (*op. cit.*, 85-86). Himu was shrewd too: "He avoided a clash with Sikandar Sur and created circumstances for a trial of strength between Sikandar and Humayun" (*op. cit.*, 86). In this regard Himu may be compared with Sher Shah, nay he even surpassed him. Himu tactfully avoided any clash with Adil Shah after assuming the title of Vikramaditya by sending presents to him. He was a ready and alert commander and helped his soldiers in any crisis. In the second battle of Panipat, when Ali Quli Khan Shaibani, who was commanding the Mughal centre, made a wide detour and extremely distressed his centre, Himu whisked to the troubled spot and tried to control the situation "making every effort to restore the battle and 'leaving no stratagem or heroic deed that his mind could conceive unattempted' (*Akbarnamah* ii 64)" (Sarker, Sir, 68).

Himu was not only commanding general but also a fighting soldier. In the Second Battle of Panipat, he dared to move to the fighting front. His capacity to tolerate physical pain was immense. In the Second Battle of Panipat, when an arrow pierced his eye, he courageously pulled it out, bandaged his eye and started giving out orders. This is really awe-inspiring. Badauni compares Himu with the legendary Rustam (Majumdar, 1984, 98), Wolseley Haig with "The barber of Tilak, who commanded the Indian cavalry of Mas'ud of Gazni" (Haig, 64), and Percival Spear calls Himu "a general of great ability" (Spear, 29). It may be noted here that Himu had the fortune to fight against both Humayun and Akbar and fought against them as "a magnificent leader" (Gascoign, 71).

Himu had great organizing power. Within a short time he could recruit a vast army. At a time when Delhi was wailing under a catastrophic famine, his army was well-supplied with victuals and provisions. It will, perhaps, not be an untruth to say that it was due to Himu's extraordinary civil and military leadership that the Afghans could keep the Mughals for some time at bay. Himu was really the hero of the Afghans and without their hero they might not have achieved as much as they had. There is a long-standing debate on the role of the hero in a mass movement. Nietzshe called the mass "a shapeless material chisel" (Progress Publishers, 1982, 399) and Carlyle, in his essay "Hero and Hero worship" was also of the same view, as was Vico who said that "all history is made by man" (Fuller, 207). Sarvepalli Radhakrishnan, in his essay "The Meaning of History", wrote: "The ancient historians of the Greco-Roman world, Thycidides, Herodotus, Tacitus, Livy, Plutarch, in spite of their aspiration to a scientific treatment of history admit that men determine history and so the study of human nature is of great importance" (Radhakrishnan, 135). Leo Tolstoy in Part II of his *War and Peace* also makes innuendoes to the same effect. But others do not agree with the view that the mass is "an infinite number of zeros" (Progress Publishers, 1982, 399). George Plekhanov dealt extensively with the problem of the place of the hero in history, in his article "On the Question of the Role of the Individual in History" (Plekhanov, 283-316), and "uses as a foil to his argument some remarks of St. Beuve, who believed that at any given moment a sudden decision of will by a great personality might redetermine the course of history" (Hook, 84). In weathering the Afghan crisis following the death of Firuz Shah (or, better, that of Islam Shah) and in promoting Afghan cause, Himu emerged a hero, changed the situation topsy turvy and re-established Afghan supremacy in Northern India, though for a brief spell of time. In this sense, R.C. Majumdar is quite right in calling Himu a hero, and in so far as Himu ultimately championed the cause of the Hindus, he was a "Hindu Hero." But in calling Himu merely a Hindu hero, *R.C. Majumdar, probably, to some extent, under-rated him, for he was not only a Hindu hero but also a Hindu King and an illustrious one at that.*

II

(As an Administrator)

Himu was not only a military genius, but also a good administrator. R.C. Majumdar says that as a *wazir* Himu was "a very capable person." (Majumdar, 1984, 94). The noted historian says that Adil Shah could well recognise "the great abilities of Himu" (*op. cit.*, 98). Himu's frequent promotions prove this amply. He helped Islam Shah in streamlining the administration. During the rule of Adil Shah, he was not only the Commander-in-Chief but also the Prime Minister plenipotentiary. Mr. Bharadwaj says that Himu "brought marked efficiency and set in order the whole paraphernalia of the Afghan administration" (Bharadwaj, 90). Himu did not tolerate corruption in administration. After occuyping Delhi, he "dismissed all the corrupt officers and replaced them by his own men (*Tarikh-i-Salatin-i-Afghana*)" (*ibid.*). Both Islam Shah and Adil Shah employed Himu in confidential positions, and Adil Shah depended chiefly on him. Himu's trustworthiness and administrative capability is attested by Edwards Thomas, for he says that Himu "was a capable [person –

SKS], as he subsequently proved himself true, and for the time he loyally upheld the fortunes of the monarch he served" (Thomas, 415). Ishwari Prasad has high praise for Himu: "His commanding talents were equally prominent in warfare and in council; and if ever one man could have kept 'Adili master of a united Afghan empire, Hemu was the man to do it" (Prasad, 190-91). At the time of Adil's ascension there were as many as five Afghan Kingdoms – *imperia in imperio* and five Afghan Kings, all of them *soi dissant*, who were unwilling to accept the overlordship of Adil (*op. cit*, 191), but Himu had the ability to iron out all recalcitrance. Internally, The Afghan soldiery was dwindled. Badaoni writes that the Afghans "lacked unity of purpose and knew little of the art of building up a permanent political organization. Even the Afghan character had deteriorated; the sense of self-respect was lowered, so much so indeed, that when Hemu charged them with cowardice they 'swallowed his insults like sweatmeats'." The Rajput soliders in his army also hated Himu for being of a *baniya* caste. And yet, with all these Afghans and Rajputs Himu won not less than ten battles, and probably as many as twenty-two battles.

Himu's administrative acumen is attested by yet another fact that "most of [The – SKS] *Jagirdars* appointed by Hemu were confirmed in their *Jagirs* by Akbar too" (Bharadwaj, 106, Appendix V). So powerful Himu, as the Prime Minister of Adil Shah, had been that Ishwari Prasad calls him the "indomitable minister" (Prasad, 226), who "displayed organizing capacity and valour of a high order" (*op. cit*, 227). Ishwari Prasad continues : "He [Hemu – SKS] was one of the greatest men of his day and among Akbar's opponents throughout Hindustan there was none who could excel him in valour, enterprise and courage" (*ibid.*). What more may one have to say in praise of an administrator?

III

(*Feeling For Fellows*)

Himu had some sympathy for the people of his own community and for his near relations. He assigned important positions to Teharpal and Ramya (in the army) who were his nephews, and also to Sangram Singh, Bhagwan Dass and others. But, perhaps, there was no stain of nepotism in all these, for, as Mr. Bharadwaj writes, he did so for overhauling the administration and banishing corruption. Referring to *Siddiqi*, Bharadwaj writes that Himu replaced *Chaudharis* and

Muqqadams and appointed Baqqals (to which community Himu belonged). This shows Himu's sympathy for his fellows even at a time when he far surpassed them all in status.

IV

(Conscious About Hindu Nationality)

Though he served the Afghan Muslims, yet in the core of his heart Himu, perhaps, did not like the Muslims – Afghan as well as Mughal. The Mughals were his enemies. On the other hand, we know that he sometimes showed hatred towards the Afghan soldiers. His hatred might have grown out of the unequal treatment shown to the Hindus by the Muslims. At the same time he had a soft corner in his heart for the Hindus. He appointed the Baqqals and other Hindus in some key positions in the administration, and his elevating his two nephews to high ranks in the army, may be construed in this line of thought. His wearing of turban in the fashion of the Ahirwals and the Rajasthanis bespeaks of his feeling of affinity with his own Hindu community. May be, he was aspiring after a unity among the Hindu populace. It may be noted here that Himu did never fight against any Hindu principality. His choice for the title of Vikramaditya also proves his affinity with the Hindus.

Some historians accuse Himu of duplicity or double-dealing for his affinity with the Hindus, and of treachery for his assuming the title of Vikramaditya and becoming an independent King. But morality in history is never independent of time. There are instances galore in medieval Indian history commensurate with what Himu did. Ala-ud-din Khilji killed his uncle-cum-father-in-law, Jalaluddin Khilji, and took up the sceptre. Aurangzeb blinded his father and captured the whole empire. So Himu's actions were not against the go of the day.

As we have seen above, Himu wanted to take away surrepticiously the political power from the Afghans and withal drive the Mughals out of India. Perhaps he was fainty conscious about the subdued surge of Hindu nationality, and we may not be far from truth if we hazard that Himu fought for this Hindu nationality.

V

(*Religion*)

Himu never forgot his religion: he was a Hindu in spirit. But we have no instance of his ill-will towards pursuants of other religions.

The religiosity of Himu was hereditary, his father being a hard-core Hindu, as we learn from his electing death instead of changing religion.

VII

(As a Man)

"Abu'l Fazl and Badauni paint the character of Himu in the blackest colour and represent him as having won the confidence of the King by ignoble means. But this is only natural for those who rightly looked upon Himu as the greatest enemy of the Mughals. But in view of the abilities displayed by Himu we should not put any faith in these slanderers" (Majumdar, 98). Again, Badauni charges Himu with brutality. He says that when Delhi and its neighbourhood was visited by a great famine, when " 'people died with the word *'bread'* upon their lips' " (*infra*), Himu "fed his five hundred elephants upon rice, sugar, and butter" (Smith, 28). But V.A. Smith writes that "The brutality of Hemu is disclosed by Badauni alone. The other historians are silent on the subject" (Smith, 28 f.n.). Further, not only Delhi and Agra but the areas under Bairam's (or Akbar's) rule were also affected by the same famine. But we do not hear that Bairam rushed victuals or any other succur to the affected areas. Besides, if Abu-l-Fazl or Badauni has to blame some one for this moral dereliction, why is it Himu and not Adil or why not both of them?

VII

(*Concluding Remarks and Heuristic Approaches*)

Barring a few Muslim historians coeval of Himu, almost all historians, medieval or modern, speak highly of Himu's qualities. The historians of the house of Tamiur accused him "of bringing number to misery [*sic*], while he pretended to be acting only from zeal for his master's service, in truth he was busy all the while enriching himself from the property of the oppressed; and by his misdeeds was whetting the axe against his master and himself" (Erskine, 491). These historians censure Himu for keeping mean company, as they suppose. They say that by distributing largesse, Himu "gained for himself a number of low and sordid adherents" (*ibid.*), who endearingly called Himu Basant Rai. But *prima facie* these charges are inimical and not evaluative. For instance, Badauni calls Himu a "foul infidel" (Prasad, 194 f.n.). Erskine counter-charges Badauni: "in spite of the prejudicial and partial representations of the historians of the house of Taimur, [Himu – SKS] must have been a man of extraordinary capacity" (Erskine, 490). R.C. Majumdar is also of the opinion that historians (Muslim) contemporary with Himu did not do justice to him. Majumdar writes: "Himu's history has been written almost wholly by his enemies who dreaded him most and, far from doing justice to his greatness, they have tarnished his name with unmerited odium" (Majumdar, 1984, 101). Majumdar (and this author) regrets the half-anonimity of Himu and feels that it "is time to resuscitate the memory and give a true account of the life of Hemchandra, really a great hero, whose dreams and achievements have been forgotten by his countrymen" (*ibid.*). Frederick Augustus also says that the Muhammedan historians have not maintained neutrality. He says that Himu "was a man of no ordinary character"; and is awe-struck at the swift vertical flight of Himu without any launching pad. Augustus writes: "Hemu was a man of no ordinary character, although his origin was obscure and his demeanour that of a veritable parvenu. Muhammedan writers, regarding him as a low-born Hindu, have represented him in an unfavourable light. His adroit and ingratiating manner won for him not only the favour but also the confidence of his Afghan masters; from his miserable rag-shop he rapidly raised himself to the influential position of bazar-overseer; he was employed with equal success in military affairs and in politics, until at length, in spite of differences of birth and creed, he became 'Adili Shah's right-hand and trusted confident. For him Hemu won battles, conquered provinces and provided the necessary men and money for every new undertaking. When he had repeatedly defeated, had expelled or killed the great Afghan chiefs of Bengal who seized these days of disturbance to attain independence, he subjugated that province in the name of his incapable master. Turning thence, he marched triumphantly north-west, leading a considerable force, to defend the interests of the house of Sur and the Afghans against the Chagatais" (Augustus, 72-73). This is rather a long quotation, but it appropriately summarizes what Himu had been. Himu united the Afghans under one umbrella; kept the redoubtable Mughals away from the Afghan domination of Northern India; nourished, imperceptibly, the Hindu revival; and ultimately founded a Hindu Kingdom; – and this Himu once used to sell salt in the winding paths of Rewari! Really, it is not for nothing that P. Kohli says that Himu "was one of the greatest men which medieval India produced" (Kohli, 1949). And let us conclude this brief annal of the legendary Himu appropriately with the words of praise for him that were produced by the facile pen of the noted historian (and the unseen inspirer of this author), R.C. Majumdar: "[Himu was – SKS] a unique episode in the history of India during Muslim rule" (Majumdar, 101).

However, further researches in the history of Himu should be done, perhaps keeping the following points in view:

(i) It is said that Himu fought and won twentytwo battles in a row. Among these only ten battles (excluding that of Panipat) have been covered by this author. Perhaps, the rest are not battles proper but skirmishes before or after some main battles. Yet the probability of these unknown battles taking place cannot be brushed aside altogether.

(ii) For further disclosure of the history of Himu more researches into Sanskrit, Persian and Urdu (the author has done some) as well as Marathi, Punjabi and other historical literary sources, should be done.

(iii) Himu's genealogy and early life, and also his personal equations should be explored further.

(iv) The social condition of the Hindus during the time of Himu should be disclosed in broader spectra.

The author is well aware of the manifold shortcomings of this dissertation, and so invites abler hands to accomplish the unaccomplished. Meanwhile, the "weary author" (*infra*) remembers what the 13th century Chinese historian Tai T'ung said —"Were I to wait perfection, my book would never be finished" (Durant, ix) — and remains.

Bibliography

(ONLY THE TITLES REFERRED TO IN THIS DISSERTATION)

English

Abu-l-Fazl, 1972, *The Akbar Nama*, *trans*. H. Beverage, Rare Books, Delhi.

Agibalova, Ye. and Donskoy, G., 1982, *History of The Middle Ages*, Progress Publishers, Moscow.

Atkinson, R.F., 1978, *Knowledge and Explanation in History*, Cornell University Press, New York.

Augustus, Frederick, 1973, *The Emperor Akbar: A Contribution Towards the History of India in the 16th Century*, *trans*. Annette S. Beveridge, vol. I, Academica Asiatica, India.

Banerjee, A.C., 1985, *History of India*, Calcutta, A. Mukherjee & Co.

Basham, A.L., 1984, *A Cultural History of India,* Delhi, Oxford University Press.

Bharadwaj, Ram Kanwar, 1975, *Hemu: A Critical Study of the Man and His Works*, Hariyana, The Rohtak Co-operative Publishing Society.

Brockelmann, Carl, 1959, *History of the Islamic Peoples*, London, Routledge & Kegan Paul.

Carter, E.H. and Mears, R.A.F., 1947, *A History of Britain*, Oxford University Press.

Datta, K.K., 1980, *Rajendra Prasad*, Publication Division, Govt. of India.

———, 1957, *A Survey of Recent Studies in Modern Indian History*, Patna, Patna University.

Davis, R.H.C., 1976, *A History of Medieval Europe*, Longman.

Davies, C. Collin, 1975, *An Historical Atlas of Indian Peninsula*, Oxford Univ. Press.

De Laet, 1957, *A Contemporary Dutch Chronicle of Mughal India*, *trans*. and ed. by Principal Brij Narain and Principal Ram Sharma, Calcutta, Susil Gupta Ltd.

Disraeli, Isaac, No date, *Curiosities of Literature*, vol. II, London, Frederick Warne & Co.

Dowson, John (ed.), 1955, *The History of India: As Told By Its Own Historians* (*The Posthumous Papers of the Late Sir H.M. Elliot*), Calcutta, Susil Gupta Ltd.

Durant, Will, 1954, *The Story of Civilization: Part I* (*Our Oriental Heritage*), New York Simon and Schuster.

Edwardes, Michael, 1967, *A History of India*, NEL Mentor Edition.

Elliot, H.M., 1964, *The History of India As Told By Its Own Historians (The Muhammedan Period)* vol. V, edited by John Dowson, Allahabad, Kitab Mahal.

———, 1955, *The History of India As Told By Its Own Historians*, edited by John Downson, Susil Gupta Ltd., Calcutta.

Erskine, William, 1972, *A History of India under the two first Sovereigns of the House of Taimur: Baber and Humayun*, vol. 2, Ireland, Irish University Press.

Ferista, Kasim, 1966, *History of the Rise of the Mahomedan Power in India Till the Year 1612*, vol. 2, *trans*. John Briggs, Calcutta, Editions Indian.

Frykenberg, R.E., 1986, *Delhi Through the Ages: Essays in Urban History, Culture and Society*, Delhi etc., Oxford University Press.

Fuller, B.A.G., *et al*, 1976, *A History of Philosophy*, Part II, New Delhi, Oxford and J.B.H.

Gascoigne, Bamber, 1971, *The Great Moghuls*, New Delhi, B.J. Publications.

Gupta, Hari Ram (ed.), 1958, *Essays Presented to Sir Jadunath Sarkar*, Hoshiarpur, Dept. of History, Punjab University.

Haig, Lt.-Colonel Sir Wolseley, 1965, *The Cambridge History of India*, vol. 3, Delhi, etc., S. Chand & Co.

———, 1971, *The Cambridge History of India*, Delhi, S. Chand & Co.

Hook, Sidney, 1943, *The Hero in History*, New Delhi, etc., Allied Publishers.

Hunter, William Wilson, 1986, *Comprehensive History of Indian Empire*, vol. 3, Delhi, Anmol Publications.

Irvine, William, 1962, *The Army of the Indian Moghuls*, New Delhi, Eurasia Publishing House.

Jouher, 1971, *The Tezekereh al Wakiat or Private Memoirs of the Moghul Emperor Humayun*, *trans*. Major Charles Stewart, Lucknow, Pustak Kendra.

Kar, Lt.-Colonel H.C., 1980, *Military History of India*, Calcutta, Firma KLM.

Khan, Ahsan Raza, 1977, *Chieftains in The Mughal Empire*, Simla, Indian Institute of Advanced Study.

Kincaid, C.A., 1968, *A History of the Maratha People*, Delhi etc., S. Chand & Co.

Kohli, P., 1949, *A History of Akbar and Mughal Administration in India*, Delhi, S. Chand & Co.

Korovkin, F., 1985, *History of the Ancient World*, Moscow, Progress Publishers.

Kulkarni, V.B., 1963, *Shivaji: The Portrait of a Patriot*, New Delhi, Orient Longmans.

Mahajan, V.D. and Mahajan, S., 1964, *Mughal Rule in India*, Delhi, S. Chand & Co.

Majumdar, R.C. (ed.), 1984, *The History and Culture of the Indian People: The Mughal Empire*, Bombay, Bharatiya Vidya Bhavan.

Majumdar, R.C., Roychaudhury, H.C. and Datta, Kalikinkar, 1967, *An Advanced History of India*, London, etc., Macmillian.

Manucci, Niccolao, 1965, *Storia Do Mogor, trans*. William Irvine, vol. I, Calcutta, Editions Indian.

Marx, K. and Engels, F., 1978, *The First Indian War of Independence*, Moscow, Progress Publishers.

Mehta, J.L., 1981, *Advanced Study in The History of Medieval India* (*The Mughal Empire 1526–1707*), New Delhi, Sterling Publishers.

Ministry of Information and Broadcasting, Govt. of India, 1982, Indian Muslims — *Proud Citizens of a Secular Country*.

Mishra, Yogendra, 1972, *The Hindu Shahis of Afghanistan and the Punjab*, Patna, Vaishali Bhavan.

Moreland, W.H. and Chatterjee, Sir. A.C., 1953, *A Short History of India*, London, etc., Longmans, Green and Co.

Mukhia, Harbans, 1976, *Historians and Historiography during the Reign of Akbar*, New Delhi, Vikas Publishing House.

Nehru, Jawaharlal, 1982, *The Discovery of India*, New Delhi, Oxford University.

Nizami, Khaliq Ahmad, 1974, *Some Aspects of Religion and Politics in India During the Thirteenth Century*, Delhi, Idarah-i-Adabiyat-i-Delhi.

Oizerman, T.J., 1986, *Principles of the Theory of the Historical Process in Philosophy, trans.* H. Campbell Crighton, Moscow, Progress Publishers.

Ojha, P.N., 1975, *North Indian Social Life*, Delhi, etc., Oriental Publishers and Distributors.

O'Leary, De Lacy, 1954, *Arabic thought and Its Place in History*, London, Routledge & Kegan Paul.

Plekhanov, Georgi, 1976, *Selected Philosophical Works*, vol. 2, Moscow, Progress Publishers.

Powell-Price, J.C., 1958, *A History of India*, London, etc., Thomas Nelson & Sons.

Prasad, Ishwari, 1975, *A Short History of The Muslim Rule in India*, Allahabad, Indian Press.

——, 1956, *The Life and Times of Humayun*, Bombay, etc., Orient Longmans.

Progress Publishers, Moscow, 1982, *The Fundamentals of Marxist-Leninist Philosophy*.

——, 1985, *A History of Afghanistan*.

Radhakrishnan, Sarvepalli, 1967, *Religion in a Changing World*, London, etc., George Allen and Unwin.

Rakitov, Anatoly, 1987, *Historical Knowledge*, *trans*. H. Campbell Creighton, Moscow, Progress Publishers.

Ranade, Justice Mahadeo Govind, 1961, *Rise of Maratha Power*, The Publication Division, Ministry of Information and Broadcasting, Govt. of India.

Ray, H.C., 1936, *The Dynastic History of Northern India* (*Early Medieval Period*), vol. 2, Calcutta University Press.

Ray Choudhury, M.L., 1951, *The State and Religion in Mughal India*, Calcutta, Indian Publicity Society.

Roychaudhury, S.C., 1984, *Social, Cultural and Economic History of India (Medieval Age)*, Delhi, Surjeet Publications.

Saksena, Banarsi Prasad, 1958, *History of Shahjahan of Delhi*, Allahabad, Central Book Depot.

Sarkar, Jagadish Narayan, 1977, *History of History in Medieval India*, Calcutta, Ratna Prakashan.

Sarkar, S.C. and Datta, K.K., 1942, *Modern Indian History*, Allahabad, Indian Press.

Sarkar, Sir Jadunath (ed.), 1977, *The History of Bengal: Muslim Period (1200–1757)*, Delhi, etc., Janaki Prakashan.

———, 1960, *Military History of India*, Calcutta, Orient Longmans.

Sastri, K.A. Nilakanta and Ramanna, H.S. 1956, *Historical Methods in Relation to Indian History*, Madras, S. Viswanathan.

Sastri, K.A. Nilakanta and Srinivasachari, G., 1986, *Advanced History of India*, New Delhi, etc., Allied Publishers.

Smith, Vincent A., 1958, *Akbar: The Great Mogul*, Delhi, S. Chand & Co.

Spear, Percival, 1985, *A History of India*, vol. 2, Penguin Books.

Srivastava, A.L., 1961, *Suja-ud-daulah*, vol. I, Delhi, etc., Shiva Lal Agarwala & Co.

Steel, (Mrs.) Flora Annie, 1919, *India Through the Ages: A Popular and Picturesque History of Hindustan*, London, George Routledge & Sons.

Stewart, Major Charles (trans.), 1971; *The Tezkereh al Wakiat*, Lucknow, Pustak Kendra.

Taylor, A.J.P., 1964, *The Origin of The Second World War*, London, Harmondsworth.

Tennyson, G.B., 1964, *A Carlyle Reader*, New York, Modern Library.

Thomas, Edward, 1967, *The Cronicles of the Patthan Kings of Delhi*, Delhi, Munshiram Manoharlal, Oriental Publishers.

Tod, Lt.-Col. James 1971, *Annals and Antiquities of Rajasthan*, vol. I, New Delhi, K.M.N. Publishers.

Tolstoy, Leo, 1972, *War and Peace*, *trans.* Constance Garnett, Pan Books.

Toynbee, Arnold, 1960, *One World and India*, Delhi, Indian Council for Cultural Relations.

Travernier, 1977, *Travels in India, trans*. V. Ball, New Delhi, Oriental Books Reprint Corporation.

Tripathi, R.P., 1956, *Rise and Fall of the Mughal Empire*, Allahabad, Central Book Depot.

Vaidya, C.V., 1986, *Downfall of Hindu India*, Delhi, Gian Publishing House.

Waley, Adolf, 1975, *A Pageant of India*, Delhi, S.P. Publications.

Weech, W.N. (ed.), 1960, *History of the World*, New Delhi, etc., Asia Publishing House.

Wolpert, Stanley, 1977, *A New History of India*, Oxford University Press.

Hindi

श्रीवास्तव, परमानन्द, *जायसी*, साहित्य अकादेमी, नई दिल्ली।

सारस्वत, रावत, प्रिथीराज रौढड, साहित्य अकादेमी, नई दिल्ली।

Journals and Encyclopaedia

The Indian Historical Review, Indian Council of Historical Research, New Delhi.

Indian Dissertation Abstracts, Indian Council of Social Science Research, New Delhi.

Journal of Indian History, The University of Kerala, Trivandrum.

Panjab University Research Bulletin, Panjab University, Chandigarh.

The New Encyclopaedia Britannica, vol. I, 1981.

INDEX

A

Adil, character of, 43-44

Afghan tribes, 26

Afghans (dominated Northern India), 32

Afghan (anti-Mguhal attitude), 78

Afghans (border Indian group), 86

Afghans (unorganized), 24

"Akbar of Kashmir" (Zainul Abedin), 20-21

Anandapala, 64, 95

Atkinson, R.F., 6-7

Aurangzeb (against the Afghans), 74

B

Babur, 13, 26-27 (Supported by the Hindus and the Afghans), 79 (poisoned by Ibrahim Lodi's mother), 79

Bajirao I, 97

Badauni, Abdul Qadir, 8

Baqqals, 106

Battle of Ghagra, 27
- Daurah, 28
- Kanauj (Bilgram), 29
- Panipat (First), 33
- Panipat (Second), 59
- Machiwara, 49, 80
- Tillepat, 59
- Khanwa, 67, 83, 96
- Sirhind, 80
- Und, 81, 95
- Tarain, 95
- Talicot, 95
- Hastings, 64
- Tours, 81
- Farra, 49

Battle-array (Second Bttle of Panipat), 60-61

Battles of Himu, 47-52

Bekasi, Mulla (as Humayun), 29, 33

Beg, Tardi, 52, 54; (execution of), 58

Bhao, Sadashivrao, 98

Bharadwaj, Ram Kanwar, 2-3, 10

Bibi Bai, 41

"bigotted Musalamn", 8

Budh, Saikh, 88

Bundella rebellion, 97

C

Consciousness of nationality, 95

Chalukyas, 95

D

Dahir, king, 65

Das, Bhagwan, 64, 66, 105

Das, Durga, 97

Das, Puran (Himu's father), 37

Deuteronomy (*The Bible)*, 83, 92

Dhimmis, 98

Diocletus, 101

Durgavati, Rani, 97

E

Edict of Nantes, 92

Emperor of Persia, 33

Epictatus, 2

execution (of Himu), 67-72

F

Farid, 25

Fazal, Abdul, 40

fanaticism, 82

Firuz (Firoze), 32 41, (murder of) 41

G

Ganesh (zaminder), 95

Gaumata, 1

Gurjara Pratiharas, 95

H

Henry IV, 92

Himu, 25, 44; (Basanta Rai or Vikramaditya or Vikramjit or Hem Chandra), 1; ("Hindu hero"), 2: (King of Delhi), 34

Himu, the Prime Minister, 34
- caste of, 36-37
- place of birth, 38-39
- picture of, 39
- appearance of, 39
- character of, 40
- "a magnificent leader", 103
- occupied the throne of Delhi, 55
- issued coins in his own name, 56
- "Hindu Hero", 56
- stories about, 62-63
- as a General, 102-4
- as an Administrator, 104-5
- feeling for fellows, 105-6
- conscious about nationality, 106
- religion of, 106-7
- as a man, 107
- high praises for, 105
- "indomitable minister", 105
- "one of the greatest men of history", 105
- (wearing a turban), 106
- man of extraordinary capacity, 108
- "one of the greatest men which medieval India produced", 108

Himu's wife, 73

Hindu state, 25

Hindu resurgency, 34

Hindu revival, 81, 86, 93-99, 108

Hindu Rastra, 97

Hindupada Padshahi, 97, 99

Hindu kingdom, 108

Hindus, 17-18, 23

Hindus (unorganised), 24

holy war (of Islam Shah), 85

Humayun, 28; (a foreigner), 30, 49

J

Jagirdars (Akbar followed Himu), 105

Jaipal, 95

Jat rebellions, 97

jauhar, 83

jihad, 82-83, 85-86, 98

Jinnatabad, 29

jiziya, 87, 90, 98

K

Kabul (Babur regarded as his home province), 30

Kamran (in the guise of a woman), 31

K..kar, Shadi Khan, 64, 66

Karrani Afghans, 26-27

Khalji, Ala-ud-din, 19, 78, 87

Khalji dynasty, 11

Khaldun, Ibn, 9

Khan, Bairam, 57

Khan, Mubariz (or Andhli or Adili), 42

Khan, Daulat, 14

Khan, Jalal (son of Sher Shah), 85

Kings of Delhi (chronology of), 25

L

Lahore, 16, 31

Lohanis, 26-27

Lodi Afghans, 10, 26

Lodi, Bahlul, 101

Lodi, Ibraham, 13

M

Mahadi movement, 31

Mahbub, 88

Majumder, R.C., 4, 54

Muhammad, Lal, 88

Mughals (foreign), 30, 33, 86, (foreign intruders) 75, 31

(organised) 24
(wiping out), 52
Muslims, (native and foreign) 78,
(marrying Hindu wives), 90, 92

N

Nagabhatta, 95
Nehru, Jawaharlal, 86
New Muslims, 79
Niazi women (maltreated), 31

P

Padmavati, 92
Palace incidence, 45
Patthans, 24
Plain of Panipat, 60
Plekhanov, George, 104
Proselytising, 90

R

Rajputs, 79, 96
Rajput women (maltreated), 31
Rakitov, Anatoly, 5-6
Ramya, 73, 105
Ratansi, 88
Rustom, 103

S

Sahia dynasty, 94
Sanga, Rana, 12, 23, 96, 102
Sastri, K.A. Nilakanta, 9
Satnami rebellion, 97
Sayyaids, 11
Second Battle of Panipat, 64-72
Shah, Sher, 26
treachery of 28, 84-85
Shah, Muhammad Adil (or Adili or Andhili), 32-33
(killed), 74, 87
Shah, Bahadur, 79
Shah, Islam, 30-32
death of, 32
picked up Himu, 32, 41-42
Shivaji, 97
Singh, Uday, 97
Singh, Man, 97
Singh, Amar, 97
Singh, Sangram, 105
Smith, V., 29
Sultanate dynasty, 11
Sur Afghans, 12
Sur dynasty, 26

T

Taylor, A.J.P., 7
Tamerlane, 81
Teharpal, 105
Temgha, 86
Tilak, 1, 103
Timur, 90-91
Timurids, 90
Tod, James, 25, 91
Toynbee, Arnold, 91
Tolstoy, 2, 10
tower (of heads), 72-73
Tughluq dynasty, 11

V

Vijoynagar Empire, 95
Vikramaditya, Raja, 54, 99
Vikramaditya (title of), 106